SCRIPT MODELS

A Handbook for the Media Writer

Robert Lee
Department of Telecommunications and Film
San Diego State University

Robert Misiorowski
Department of Telecommunications and Film
San Diego State University

Communication Arts Books

HASTINGS HOUSE, PUBLISHERS
New York 10016

We wish to express our appreciation to the following
contributors:

Fred Ashman, Managing Director, Multi Image Productions,
        San Diego, for his permission to include excerpts
        from his Western Airlines multimedia script.

Carolyn Lee, artist, San Diego, for her Steinman Sure-Stop
        commercial storyboard.

Len Levy, Executive Producer, Foote, Cone & Belding/Honig,
        Los Angeles, for his permission to include the
        Mazda "RX3-SP" commercial.

Robert McKee, Assistant Professor, Department of Telecom-
        munications and Film, San Diego State University,
        for his permission to include his teleplay pilot,
        It's the Law, "A Horse of a Different Color".

Denis Sanders, writer-producer-director, and President,
        SRS Productions, Inc., Los Angeles, for his
        permission to include the concept for
        Czechoslovakia, 1968.

Second Printing, August 1979

Library of Congress Cataloging in Publication Data

Lee, Robert, 1925–   Script models.

  (Communication arts books)
  Bibliography: p.
  1. Mass media—Authorship.   2. Mass Media—Handbooks, manuals, etc.
I. Misiorowski, Robert, joint author.   II. Title.
P91.L35   808′.066′791   78-1267
ISBN 0-8038-6755-7
ISBN 0-8038-6754-9 pbk.

Published simultaneously in Canada by Copp Clark Ltd., Toronto
Printed in the United States of America

TABLE OF CONTENTS

Introduction   6

PART I <u>Scripts and Scripting</u>

Filmstrips:

    A note about the filmstrip   9
    Silent filmstrip teaching guide sample   10-11
    Sound filmstrip script sample   12-13

Multimedia:

    A note about the multimedia script   14
    Script sample   15-17

Non-Theatrical Motion Pictures:

    Cover sheet   20
    Proposals and treatments
      A note about proposals and treatments   18
      Proposal/premise sample   19
      Treatment sample   19
      Concept sample   20-28
    Scripts
      Documentary
        A note about the visual documentary form   29
      Technical/Instructional
        A note about the technical/instructional
          script form   30
        Technical/Instructional script sample   31-33
    Storyboards
      A note about storyboards   75
      Storyboard example   77

3

Theatrical Motion Pictures:

    Cover sheet   40
    Proposals and treatments
        A note about treatments and outlines   34
        Treatment sample   35
    Scripts
        A note about theatrical motion picture scripts   37
        Format for teleplays/screenplays   38
        Screenplay model   39
        Teleplay/screenplay sample   40-42
        Master scene script sample   43-44
    Storyboards
        A note about storyboards   75
        Storyboard example   77

Television:

    Cover sheets
        Comedy series cover sheet   50
        Teleplay cover sheet   58
    Proposals and treatments
        A note about treatments and outlines   34
        Teleplay outline sample   36
    Scripts
        Comedy Series
            A note on television comedy series scripts   45
            Format for television comedy series scripts   46-47
            Comedy series script model   48-49
            Comedy series script sample   50-52
        Commercial/PSA
            A note about the TV commercial/public
               service announcement script forms   53
            Shared-ID script sample   54
            Public service spot sample   55
            Product commercial script samples   56, 76
        One- and Two-Column
            A note about the one- and two-column scripts   57
            One-column script sample   58-61
            Two-column script sample   62-64
        Teleplay/Screenplay
            Format for teleplays/screenplays   38
            Teleplay model   39
            Teleplay/screenplay sample   41-42
            Master scene script sample   43-44
    Storyboards
        A note about storyboards   75
        Storyboard example   77

Radio:

Scripts
    A note about the drama/documentary
      production script   65
    Format for production scripts   66
    Production script model   67
    Production script sample   68-69
    Dialogue commercial sample   70
    News copy sample (see "Straight announce copy")
    Straight announce copy sample   71

PART II   <u>Writers' Aids</u>

Storyboards
    A note about storyboards   75
    Product commercial script from which the
      storyboard example was developed   76
    Storyboard example   77

Timing tips   78

Protecting the property: copyright and
  registration   79-80

Agents   81

Suggestions from the professionals   82

Readings for writers
    Books   83-84
    Periodicals   85-86

Glossary   87-96

INTRODUCTION

This booklet is designed to provide a resource for writers commencing work in radio, television and film. For the observant, it will function as more than a reference. This may be especially true as regards the Glossary. The quickest way to become acquainted with a new field is to become familiar with its vocabulary. Thus, a glossary is not merely a collection of definitions; it maps the field--its range, its way of functioning, the materials and characteristics peculiar to it. We therefore urge, as the first step in writing for media, a thoughtful reading of our Glossary.

The script examples included in this booklet illustrate most of the situations the media writer is apt to encounter. The writer must choose the form most capable of conveying ideas toward his expressive ends, and must understand who the first reader will be. The first reader is seldom the director who will translate written phrases into images or sound patterns; it is more likely to be an intermediary between the writer and that director. (The script will have to be sold first, and only later can it be produced!) We stress this to admonish writers to keep their scripts as lean as possible, to avoid "directing the program from the typewriter" (by overspecifying instructions of whatever kind), and to make the script as easy to read as possible.

A script's value is as a communication tool: it allows understanding among several diverse departments and many specialists--all of them with different interests and functions. This is true of all script forms; they have in common that they must contain all the information needed by the parties who will come together to give substance to a final product.

PART I

Scripts and Scripting

A note about the filmstrip: This is a persistent
form; it has weathered the impact of increased film
production and the advent of the filmograph. A series
of still photos or other graphics copied onto contin-
uous 35mm stock, the filmstrip has clear advantages
over the motion picture: its frames are advanced one
at a time, usually at will, for detailed study, and
its accompanying explanatory text can be quite easily
modified, updated, matched to another target audience,
etc. Filmstrips tend to be accompanied by sound--
often, by a composite of dialogue, narration, music
and effects--in the form of cassettes, open reel tapes,
or discs. Some projecting systems are triggered by
subaudible tones, and so change frames automatically,
in synchronization with the sound. Other systems
feature audible tones which signal the operator to
change frames manually. But many are more basic
still, relying upon an operator not only to change
frames, but to read from a prepared "script," or
teaching guide. These silent filmstrips are not only
less expensive, but allow closer tailoring by a presenter for his audience and a pacing to suit its
learning and comprehension levels. Further, the
teaching guide itself may contain a brief abstract
for a given frame (the "A" copy) as well as a more
involved or an elaborating commentary (the "B" copy);
the operator can read either, or both, depending upon
his audience.

One of the following examples illustrates this
form. Its companion represents the sound filmstrip
form. Both scripts deal with the same subject (their
visuals are identical); a comparative study is urged.

(Silent Filmstrip Teaching Guide Script Sample)

Frame # 1.   TITLE: "How Far is Up?   The Airport Crunch"

Frame # 2.   TITLE: "Produced in Cooperation with the Federal Aviation Agency"

Frame # 3.   TITLE: "A Pathfinder Production"

Frame # 4.   PHOTO: A 747 jetliner flying overhead.

> A) Each year in the United States, there are 1,465,920 commercial flights in and out of our ten busiest airports.
>
> B) 205,062,000 passengers each year fly into these major airports aboard commercial carriers.

Frame # 5.   PHOTO: An "elephant parade" of many airliners awaiting takeoff.

> A) The "elephant parade," the long line waiting to take off, exemplifies the problem with commercial air carriers. Here is the aviation bottle-neck.
>
> B) The problem is not in the air; once aloft, there is little crowding along the well-controlled air lanes. Around airports, the situation is compounded by an additional 3,109,800 flights other than airlines, at our ten busiest airports.

Frame # 6.   ARTWORK: A modification of the previous picture; the airplane frames now resemble automobiles.

> If auto passengers had to contend with the same traffic situation, on a per-500-person basis, our highway system could not function.

Frame # 7.   PHOTO: Atlanta Airport, with identifying caption.

A) Atlanta, Georgia is the fifth busiest airport in America.   469,500 air operations a year jam its facility.

B) The Atlanta airport was built in the late 1940's and its modifications were largely determined by encroaching neighboring build-up.

Frame # 8.   GRAPH: Depiction of Atlanta traffic -- airline flights, 414,544 (88.2%); general aviation, 44,606 (9.5%); air taxi flights, 9,260 (1.9%); military flights, 1,088 (-%).

Atlanta's percentage of airline flights, in relation to its other traffic, is the highest such percentage among the nation's ten leading airports.

(etc., etc.)

11

(Sound Filmstrip Sample)

Frame #1.
   TITLE: "How Far is
   Up? The Airport
   Crunch"

(Music: theme.)

Frame #2.
   TITLE: "Produced in
   Cooperation with the
   Federal Aviation
   Agency"

Frame #3.
   TITLE: "A Pathfinder
   Production"

(Music cross-fade to jet sound.)

Frame #4.
   PHOTO: 747 jet fly-
   ing overhead.

NARRATOR: The modern airliner is
a marvelous way of travel. Great
for businessmen, easy for vacation-
ers. Coast-to-coast in half a
workday.

Frame #5.
   PHOTO: An "elephant
   parade" of many air-
   liners waiting to
   take off.

The problem is getting up into the
sky. Or getting down out of it.
The bottle-neck is our airports.

(Jet sound cross-fade to auto horns
bleating.)

Frame #6.
   ART: Same as #5, but
   jets are ghostly, and
   their frames are re-
   enforced as cars, and
   extending back into
   infinity.

NARRATOR: If automobiles faced the
same traffic situation -- per 500
people carried -- freeways would be
immobilized.

(Music: background.)

Frame #7.
   PHOTO: Atlanta air-
   port. (Caption: "At-
   lanta")

NARRATOR: Atlanta, Georgia is the
fifth busiest airport in America.
470-thousand air operations a year
jam its facility.

Frame #8.
   GRAPH: As per nar-
   ration.

Atlanta's heavy traffic is 88-percent
airline, 9-and-a-half percent general
aviation, 2-percent air taxi. The
remainder is military aviation.
(PAUSE)

12

Frame #9.
   ART: Concept of
super airport with
shuttle service.

One proposed solution to Atlanta's
congestion may lie in such a layout
as this. The green area is reserved
for airline operations, and conveyor
systems speed passengers to and from
their planes.

Frame #10.
   PHOTO: Passengers
hurrying through a
terminal.

(Music: a frantic burst.)

NARRATOR: Travellers have been sub-
jected to too much of this.

Frame #11.
   PHOTO: Another view
of hurrying travel-
lers.

(Music subsides into background.)

Frame #12.
   PHOTO: O'Hare Air-
port. (Caption:
"Chicago")

NARRATOR: Nearly 670-thousand
flights a year come into and out of
Chicago's O'Hare -- 50-thousand
flights busier than America's second
busiest airport.

(etc., etc.)

(etc., etc.)

13

A note about the multimedia script: Multimedia presentations have gained a strong position among audio-visual methods. The medium is so recent, a specific script form has not yet emerged. The medium itself employs several screens and often many motion picture and slide projectors operating simultaneously.

In the following example, not one of his most elaborate multimedia presentations, Fred Ashman used three screens to reflect pictures from one motion picture projector and nine slide projectors. From the script, a detailed "shot sheet" was derived and the visuals recorded according to its stipulations.

(Multimedia Script Sample)

WESTERN AIRLINES MASTER SCRIPT: FINAL DRAFT (RECORDED)
                                  DRAFT 6
              "NEW LOOK '76"

house lights fade red logos on black	tympani roll
WAL logos animated	anncr: LADIES AND GENTLEMEN / WESTERN AIRLINES VERY PROUDLY WELCOMES YOU TO WESTERN'S WORLD, AND ALL THE SERVICE, CONVENIENCE AND EXCITEMENT THAT GOES WITH IT.
montage of WAL cities and service	music in strong
panorama of key cities	anncr: WESTERN'S WORLD IS MAGNIFICENT.........
panorama	IT'S BREATHTAKING......
panorama	AND IT'S INVITING......

15

                              WESTERN IS AMERICA'S SENIOR AIRLINE,

shots of cities
                              SERVING THE WESTERN WORLD IN 41 CITIES,

Canada and Mexico
                              FIFTEEN STATES, CANADA AND MEXICO.

all slow fade to black   THAT'S A LOT OF PEOPLE TO SERVICE

people montage   BUT AT WESTERN, SERVING PEOPLE IS WHAT

                              WE'RE ALL ABOUT...

people...all sizes,
                              music in strong

shapes, ages, races

/ /

WESTERN AIRLINES '76

San Diego scenes   anncr: RETURNING NORTH WE FIND

OURSELVES IN SAN DIEGO, A FAST

DEVELOPING FAMILY RESORT CENTER....

WHERE CALIFORNIA BEGINS.../

Los Angeles   anncr: THE SPRAWLING GIANT,

LA Harbor   LOS ANGELES. TRULY A GATEWAY CITY,
Queen Mary
Century City   LOS ANGELES HAS MANY FASCINATING FACES.
Studio shots
Beverly Hills   BEVERLY HILLS, PASADENA, NEWPORT BEACH,
Newport Beach-Harbor
Surfing   ALL ARE A PART OF THIS THRIVING AREA./
Western Headquarters
Western DC-10 hanger   LOS ANGELES IS HEADQUARTERS FOR

WESTERN'S WORLD, / AND SOME OTHER

Disneyland   WORLDS TOO./

Disney music

17

A note about non-theatrical motion picture proposals and treatments: Some statement of the purpose, aims, length, methodology and cost of a film or other media work must usually be presented prior to embarking upon the development of the treatment and script. This is the function of an initial document which we refer to as a proposal, although it is sometimes called a premise. This presentation often includes a section where the officer of the funding organization indicates his acceptance of the proposal, and so the document also serves as an informal contractual agreement.

After the proposal is accepted, a treatment, a more lengthy document which generally details the progression of the intended presentation from beginning to end, is prepared. This document is often developed from an outline or sequence outline. Sometimes the treatment includes specific camera shots, pieces of narration, a description of the necessary graphics, an idea of the animated sequences, etc. Once the treatment is approved the script may be developed or, in many cases, the shooting will be started. In this case, the script will be written after the specific visuals are screened for the writer, producer and client.

While the proposal and treatment are usually separate elements of pre-production, occasionally a hybrid form, called a concept, may be used. This is especially true when the client approaches the producer/writer with a pre-conceived idea for a project.

In the excellent example of a concept by Denis Sanders and Robert Fresco, eight pages of poetic vision--a statement of how they foresaw their short documentary film dealing with the rape of a nation--was presented to their client, the United States Information Agency. Their concept indicates a plan for a motion picture which would evoke feelings rather than present explicit facts. The film which finally emerged spoke eloquently--and wholly without narration--of the disconsolate history of Czechoslovakia. Released for theatrical exhibition by special dispensation of the U.S. Congress, Czechoslovakia, 1968 received an Academy Award.

(Non-Theatrical Motion Picture Proposal/Premise Sample)

This proposal is for a 25 minute color sound motion picture in 16mm, intended to make audiences aware of aviation as a significant accomplishment of man, and to convey certain of its principles. Where live photography cannot tell the story, animation can be used. The estimated cost of the production is $18,000. Following a brief introduction by U.S. Air Chief of Staff, the first pioneering attempts will be shown. Upon arrival at modern principles of flight, aerodynamic physics is treated in a very basic manner and simply. A number of filmclips from Wright-Patternson wind-tunnel tests can be used in this section to supplement. . . (etc.)

(Non-Theatrical Motion Picture Treatment Sample)

Over a black screen, we hear the approach of an early airplane engine; when sound is well-established, a very slow fade-in reveals a 1923 Jenny. Main titles, in a masculine font, appear after several seconds, accompanied by march music. After titles, we hold on the Jenny, then dissolved to a model of the same aircraft on the desk of the Air Chief of Staff, whom we pan up to reveal. He explains that the conquest of the air has been no miracle --that man has endured much for its sake, and progress has come piece by piece with the efforts and sacrifice of countless men . . . (etc.)

. . . As the P-51 levels out of its searing dive we "freeze" it, then optically zoom in on it moderately fast; toward the end of the zoom, we dissolve to an animation drawing of a P-51. As the narrator discusses each part of the plane, that part changes color for added emphasis...(etc.)

(Cover Sheet Sample. With appropriate changes, this form is proper also for non-theatrical motion picture proposals, treatments, and scripts.)

(16th line)   <u>CZECHOSLOVAKIA: 1968</u>

(21st line)   Concept for a

                     one-reel

                     motion picture

                     for

                     The United States Information Agency

(43rd line)   Denis Sanders
                                     Robert M. Fresco
                                     1234 Pico Street
                                     Los Angeles, Calif.
                                     90028
(48th line)   November 11, 1968   **213-555-4321**

Preface

    The callous invasion of August 20, 1968, seems to us much
more than simply another Czech disaster--

    Or simply an invasion at all.

    August 20th seems but the latest step in a macabre dance in
which the Czech people have been whirled since 1918, the year
they declared themselves a republic.

    There appears, in our view, a horrifying rhythm:

    From shadow to liberty, they dance... again into shadow, then
brief liberty, and shadow once again.

    A last, brief flourish of liberty, and then--

    August 20th, 1968.

    It is a sadly poetic cycle, seemingly without end, and our
intent is to present it as such.

    To enclose the factual within the emotional. To impart our
message as much through style and mood as through the inclusion of
any orderly specifics--though they exist, and are used.

    A note on style:

    If this short film is to succeed with worldwide audiences,
then it must belong to itself--be as original--as those films
which so distinguished Expo '67 and the New York World's Fair,
some of the best of which, ironically enough, were Czech. Thus,
the following approach. And if, at first glance, it seems
startling, be comforted:

    The shape springs completely from content--and ourselves.

CZECHOSLOVAKIA: 1968

The Cast:

    1.   The people and events of Czechoslovakia from 1918 through 1968 as recorded on motion picture film and stills.

    2.   Color photography.

    3.   Black-and-white photography.

    4.   One 35mm Slide Projector, always seen in black-and-white.

The Message:

"The Lights Went Out. . ."

FADE IN:

A Slide Projector comes to life, in black-and-white, turned on by an unseen hand. The light flares, the cooling fan whirs, and now the automatic slide holder begins to revolve, clicking forward at its automatic and pre-set intervals.

The first slide has not yet arrived before the lens. We watch closely as it advances, pauses, advances, pauses, until we see that it is there. This first slide and the next three are in color, and carry the legend:

Czechoslovakia: 1968

--in dozens of languages.

Again the slide projector, as the next slide advances and arrives, also in color:

<u>1918</u>

What follows--in sixty seconds--is Czechoslovakia as it is for some twenty years: 1918 and onwards, seen in color stills and tinted motion picture film:

Czechoslovakia's countryside, bursting with flowers. Its peoples, its cities, its rivers and castles, its street life and budding industry--and, always and again, its <u>flowers</u>.

In fact, it is a picture of beautiful flowers which ends our sequence: flowers turning before us from color to black-and-white, followed then by a black-and-white slide:

<u>1938</u>

More flowers--on a grave, now.

The Nazi occupation, in grim black-and-white. We watch the destruction, the tears, and the drawn and terrible faces of the Czechs as they are violated.

Mercilessly, our projector clicks on, mercilessly parading these faces before us.

Then, as we watch the last face, it floods with <u>color</u>--and we switch brightly to our next slide:

1948

Flowers, proffered traditionally, warmly--to Russians.

Czech life from their liberation in 1945 to the Communist takeover of 1948, compressed in a bright, colorful swirl:

Street scenes, gaiety, shops, much activity--

Which chills into a black-and-white gloom as Czechoslovakia's freedom is once again taken from her.

Taken from within.

A defilation aided, as we watch, not by her enemies but by her deliverers.

Once again, the flowers of pain.

And the stark black-and-white slide:

1968

Once again, a change, as the numbers on the slide go slowly from black-and-white to color...

Czechoslovakia--in color--as a modest liberalization slowly gathers confidence, and grows:

Magazine stands, selling periodicals from the world over-- including the West. Shops, filling. Students, smiling. Flowers, of course. And jazz clubs, and dancing, and--

Black-and-white Russians at Cierna.

Dubcek, in _color_. Becoming Dubcek in black-and-white.

In Prague, demonstrations of support, in <u>color</u>.

Dubcek--gaining color, smiling, responding to the Czech's acclaim and relief, smiling--smiling, with a smiling Breshnev accepting a Czech welcome at his side.

Suddenly, Prague is black-and-white.

The black-and-white troops and tanks and aircraft of Soviet intervention...

The black-and-white fear, and then bewilderment, and then, quickly, the resistance of the Czechs:

Young and old, attacking the Soviet tanks...

Busses, used to block their way...

The outbursts of a newly-violated people:

Demonstrations against the occupiers--Confrontations, face to face--Street signs disappear--Underground newspapers flourish--Clandestine radio stations counsel the populace--

There are clashes--

There are screams--

There is a general strike--

There is silence...

Click. The projector's continuing click.

The Russians are angry.

The Russian answer is might, and death. And we see, once

more--flowers.

But these are flowers placed upon bloodstained cobblestones.

Upon coffins.

And in graveyards...

The slide projector continues to click grimly on:

Black-and-white Prague.

Black-and-white Czechs. Black-and-white Dubcek. Black-and-white city squares, and shops...

And masses of black-and-white flowers, piled at the black-and-white funeral of a young girl.

Masses of flowers. Black-and-white flowers...

Again, the projector, its carriage advancing. One... two... three...

And once more, we re-live our opening:

Once again, in color, the slides come:

Czechoslovakia: 1968

--in dozens of languages.

Once again, the year:

1918

Once again, Czechoslovakia in her first freedom:

The same scenes of Prague and the people and the Czech countryside.   And the flowers--bursting with color.

The flowers.

That turn black-and-white...

We return to our black-and-white slide projector.

And as we watch and hear the carriage click forward, as the
slides of Czechoslovakia's story come marching into place at their
automatic and pre-set intervals...

We very briefly SUPERIMPOSE the necessary credits--

And FADE OUT.

27

Film and Still references

    The "Greek" material.

    Visnews.

    Grimberg Library (ABC and Pathe).

    Magnum Photos.

    The Concerned Photographer Exhibit
      --Cornell Capa, Director

    UPI.

    Others.

Sound references

  FX:

    The actual and sometimes exaggerated sounds of a
large, heavy-duty carousel slide projector.

    No other FX--not screaming, nor crowds, nor tanks.

  Music:

    An original score of five to seven minutes duration.

A note about the visual documentary form: Since there
are several documentary "modes" and approaches, there cannot
be only one script form. A documentary which relies upon
archive footage (library shots), might make do with a simple
listing of the shots needed. A cinéma vérité documentary
might go into production with only a treatment or an out-
line--or an idea. The Theatrical Screenplay Model is
appropriate for the dramatized documentary, where visual
and aural elements are known in advance and can be planned
for in the same way as for a directed drama. The Technical/
Instructional Model may be used for the documentary as well,
if it is kept in mind that documentary shooting cannot be so
fastidiously planned in advance. The kind of "script" chosen
for a documentary, then, will ultimately depend upon the kind
of documentary being considered. For this reason no one
sample is included.

A note about the technical/instructional film script
form: This is used in situations where the assignment is
tightly circumscribed and details carefully authorized, and
where, for reasons of authenticity and accuracy, interpre-
tive freedom during shooting or later production phases
cannot be practiced. Once the script has been cleared
through advisors, the film is shot as closely as possible
to that script, and all post-production elements are made
to correspond closely with it. It therefore represents a
cinema form in which the script dictates rather than guides.

(Technical/Instructional Script Sample)

Action:	Sound:
	Early vintage engine (prefer- ably an OX-5) fades in slowly, holds.
FADE IN slowly on:	
1. 1923 Jenny, flying through cloudy sky.	
SUPERIMPOSE:	
1x. Title. "Natura Films Presents"	**Music:**
	In with a swelling roar, a march expressing man's triumph over the air. Holds until action fade out, then out.
DISSOLVE to:	
1y. Title: "Flight"	
DISSOLVE to:	

1z. Title: "Produced by Denis
    Shotts in Cooperation with
    the United States Air Force"	

(etc., etc., other titles)	
FADE OUT titles and maintain as in Sc. 1.	
DISSOLVE to:	
2a. Interior Day. CU Jenny Model on deck.	
TILT UP to:	

2b. MS General Smith.
    He sits behind the desk,
    reading some papers.	

He puts down papers, removes his glasses as he looks up at camera.	**Gen. Smith:**
	As Chief of Staff for the United States Air Force, I can say unqualifiedly (etc.) As a pilot of our nation's aircraft since 1927, I have seen phenomenal progress in aviation.
DOLLY BACK to:	
2c. MLS Gen. Smith	I have seen aircraft grow in strength, in speed, in carry- ing capacity. I have seen their appearances change from
He reaches out and picks up Jenny model.	this frail (MORE)

	<u>Gen. Smith</u> (cont.):
3. CU Jenny model.	1923 Jenny, which gave us so much service, to that of
4. MCU Frames photo of FB-111 on wall of Gen. Smith's office (established in Sc. 2c or 2b). (etc., etc.)	our latest tactical jet bomber: FB-111. (etc., etc.)

/ /

	<u>Narrator</u> (VO): . . . is the job of the ailerons.
28. Flaps.	
After very brief hold, they change suddenly from grey to green.	An additional surface must be provided to add further lift to the aircraft:
Pop on "Flaps"	Flaps. Since this additional lift is needed only during take-offs and landings--and would retard the aircraft in normal flight--
Flaps move from down to up.	the flaps are retractable.
29a. Elevators.	
After very brief hold, they change suddenly from grey to green.	Another of the aircraft's control surfaces is the elevator area. Unlike the ailerons, the elevators move together. . .
Elevators move up.	either up. . .
Elevators move down.	or down. In <u>this</u> position, air-- (MORE)
DOLLY BACK to:	
29b. MLS Tail section of aircraft.	

(29b continued)

Air--red strands--
enters frame and
moves the tail up.

Air dissipates and
elevators return to
"up" position.

Air--red strands--
enters frame again;
this time moving tail
down.

FADE OUT:
FADE IN on:

30. LS F-15 during acro-
    batics.
    It levels off and dives.

DISSOLVE to:

31. Model in wind tunnel.

(etc.)

Narrator (VO)(cont.):

passing over the surface--
pushes the tail up and, so,
the nose down...and the
aircraft dives.

With the elevators up, the
tail is pushed down...

the nose rises . . . and the
plane climbs.

Sound:

Shriek of jet engine; then
take under narrator. On
action dissolve, cross-fade
to rush of wind.

Narrator (VO):

Now, what happens in super-
sonic flight situations?
This question must be
answered before the air-
craft is built. That is

the purpose of the wind
tunnel.

(etc.)

33

(Set pica tabs at:)

12   21   37   46   55   73

<u>A note about the theatrical motion picture treatment
and television outline</u>: In essence, the treatment, or
outline, is a short story running from ten to sixty pages
which describes the progress of the story idea from first
scene to last. Written in the present tense, it details
all the characters and their general actions, indicates
the interrelationships among the characters, shows the
dramatic progression, gives any important camera directions, and may include specific lines of dialogue.
Beginning writers are encouraged to use the treatment to
work up their ideas and then develop the script form
from it.

Professionally, a treatment may be purchased and then
discussed and modified by the producer, studio, etc., in
a series of story conferences. When the final story is
solidified, work begins on the script itself. A beginning
writer, however, should be aware that if he submits a
treatment which is purchased, it is likely to be developed
by someone whose scriptwriting abilities are better known
to the producer. For the novice, the surest way to get a
screen credit is to submit the script itself.

(8th line)   RIGHT UP FRONT

(11th line)   A Treatment for a Screenplay
(13th line)   by
(15th line)   Zaven Yuralian

(19th line)   The landscape of central Arizona flashes by.
A drunken hand thrusts a glass into the frame and a
voice offers it to ROBIN BALLARD. She refuses the
offer with cold detachment and continues to stare
blankly through the window of the club car. She is
a delicate woman whose thirty years are reflected
in the stress-filled face which stares back from
the image in the glass.

At Union Station in Los Angeles, Robin frantically
searches the crowd. She calms and her face brightens
as LAUREN CHANDLER hurries to join her. Lauren,
Robin's mother, is a beautiful woman in her mid-fifties,
self-possessed, a woman of the world. She comforts
her anxious daughter and asks what is wrong. Robin
reveals that she has left her brutal husband. Lauren
is confused and says that Tom, Robin's husband, is
waiting for them in the parking lot. Robin is begging
Lauren to sneak her out of the station, when a man's
voice calls her name. Panicked, she pulls away from
her mother and runs down the platform.

(8th line)   <u>"Terror on the 'B' Train"</u>

(11th line)   An Outline for a 1-Hour Teleplay

(13th line)   by

(15th line)   Zaven Yuralian

(17th line)   1/1/77

(21st line)   <u>TEASER</u>

(24th line)   The scene is a crowded subway platform in New York City. Tired commuters joust for positions close to the edge, faces are drawn, jackets hang from shoulders, shirt sleeves are rolled up. The train roars into the station, dust flying. As it slows, the crowd shifts. The train stops, but the doors don't open. Suddenly a voice cries that the passengers on the train are all dead. People scream and panic. Slowly the doors open and a cloud of gas escapes from the train. Holding their hands over their noses, the bystanders scatter from the platform in terror. Inside the train, the passengers are slumped in their seats, the floor is littered with bodies. Nothing

(50th line)   lives, absolute silence, as we fade to black.

(53rd line)   <u>ACT ONE</u>

(56th line)   Policemen crowd the platform. LIEUTENANT KOPECKY, a burly, gruff, no-nonsense veteran, questions etc.

A note about theatrical motion picture scripts: The language of Hollywood has lost its death-grip on screenwriting. Once a document which specified every change in angle, and which numbered these as scenes (as in production-ready shooting scripts), the screenplay today is looser, more readable, and tends to use master scenes, or scene descriptions, rather than camera directions. An example of this newer method, the screen directions or master scene form, is included in this booklet; it should be compared with the more traditional Teleplay/Screenplay Sample.

The Format For Teleplays/Screenplays

1. Camera shots are numbered on both sides of each page on the heading line. They are numbered consecutively.

2. Camera directions, scene descriptions, and stage directions are typed within the margins of 20 and 73 pica spaces.

3. Dialogue is typed within the margins of 30 to 65 pica spaces. Name of the speaking character heads (in UPPER CASE) his lines of dialogue. Instructions as to how lines are to be delivered (lamely, resigned, furious, whispering) are placed on parentheses on line beneath the character's name and 5 spaces to the left.

4. Use UPPER CASE for:

   INT. or EXT., at heading of scene,
   INDICATION OF PLACE, at heading of scene,
   INDICATION OF DAY OR NIGHT, at heading of scene,
   NAMES OF CHARACTERS (JEROME, KANE, POLICEMAN,
      PASSERBY) when first introduced in the stage
      directions, and to indicate their dialogue,
   CAMERA ANGLES and CAMERA DIRECTIONS, and
   SCENE TRANSITION DEVICES, if they must be
      specifically stated.

5. Use single spacing for:

   Dialogue,
   Camera movements and angles,
   Stage directions,
   Scene descriptions,
   Sound or effects cues.

6. Use double spacing to separate:

   A camera shot from the next camera shot,
   A scene from any interceding transition (FADE OUT/
      FADE IN, DISSOLVE TO),
   The speech of one character from the heading of the
      next character, and
   A speech from a camera or stage direction.

(Theatrical Screenplay Model)

(line 7)   <u>ACT ONE</u>

                               (Use this heading in teleplay
                               but not in screenplay format)

(line 12)   FADE IN:

(line 14) 1. EXT. OR INT. - INDICATION OF WHERE SCENE TAKES PLACE - 1.
                 TIME SCENE TAKES PLACE (DAY, NIGHT, LATER, SAME) -
                 CAMERA'S ANGLE OF VIEW AND SUBJECT COVERED (IF INCLUDED).

                 Description of the setting, CHARACTERS, and action
                 taking place in the scene are written within these
                 margins. All sounds except speech are contained
                 in this space as well.

                             NAME OF CHARACTER
                          (the way he delivers the
                          line: inflections, tone)
                     His line occupies the space to here.

                             CHARACTER TWO
                     May have a line at this point.
                          (if his tone changes,
                          indicate so here)
                     All dialogue occurs within this
                     space.

                 Transitional devices between scenes are indicated,

                                                        (TRANSITION:)

           2. EXT. OR INT.   SAME AS ABOVE   2.

                 And the next scene begins. The second time a
                 Character is mentioned, the name is not put in
                 upper case. If you come to the bottom of the
                 page and the scene continues, indicate it,

                                                        (CONTINUED)

           /

(line 6) 2. CONTINUED: 2.

(line 8)   like this. Whenever possible, avoid splitting
                 dialogue from page to page.

(Set pica tabs as:)
          15 20   30   35   40   68   75   79

(Line 25)   RIGHT UP FRONT

(Line 29)   A Screenplay

(Line 31)   by

(Line 33)   Zaven Yuralian

(Line 36)   Based on a Story

(Line 38)   by

(Line 40)   Susan Lucas

(Line 53)   FIRST DRAFT   Represented by:
                 January 1, 1977
                                             Acme Associates
                                             421 Fairfax Lane
                                             Los Angeles, Calif. 90013

                                             (213)555-1944

FADE IN:

1.   INT.   CLUB CAR OF MOVING TRAIN   DAY   1.

The desert landscape of central Arizona flashes by
outside the window. A cocktail glass, held by a
MAN'S shaky hand, is thrust into the frame.

                    MAN'S VOICE
                    (slurred)
            Buy you a drink, pretty lady?

The CAMERA PULLS BACK to reveal ROBIN BALLARD, a
delicate, thirty-year-old woman. She is under
a great deal of strain.

                    ROBIN
                 (coldly, without
                  looking at him)
        No.

The drink is pulled out of the frame.

                    MAN'S VOICE
                  (sarcastically)
            Well, pardon me.

Robin continues to stare out the window. The CAMERA
ZOOMS IN on her reflection in the window which returns
her vacant gaze.

                                        DISSOLVE TO:

2.   EXT.   UNION STATION, LOS ANGELES   DAY   2.
        ESTABLISHING SHOT

The passengers stream out of the train and are
greeted by friends.

CUT TO:

3.   MED. SHOT — ROBIN   3.

She frantically searches the crowded platform.
She stops and her face brightens as she recognizes
someone.

                                        (CONTINUED)

3.   CONTINUED: 3.

                                 ROBIN
                             (waving)
           MOM.
                           (calls louder)
           MOM!

CUT TO:

4.   ROBIN'S POV   4.

as LAUREN CHANDLER, a beautiful, fifty year old, self-possessed woman, hears Robin's call and spots her. Lauren waves and hurries toward Robin.

CUT TO:

5.   TWO SHOT - ROBIN AND LAUREN   5.

The women embrace. Robin starts to cry.

                             LAUREN
                       (very concerned)
         Baby, baby.
                   (beat)
        What's the matter?

FADE IN:

1.   INT.   CLUB CAR OF MOVING TRAIN   DAY   1.

The desert landscape of central Arizona flashes by
outside the window. A drunken MAN staggers up the
aisle holding a cocktail glass. He notices
ROBIN BALLARD, a delicate, thirty year old woman,
who stares blankly out the window. He holds the
glass out to her.

                         MAN
                      (slurred)
           Buy you a drink, pretty lady?

Robin continues to stare out the window.

                         ROBIN
                      (coldly)
           No.

The Man pulls back the drink.

                         MAN
                   (sarcastically)
           Well, pardon me.

He turns and walks away. Robin's reflection in the
window returns her gaze.

2.   EXT.   UNION STATION, LOS ANGELES   DAY   2.

Robin, surrounded by other disembarking passengers,
frantically searches the crowded platform. She brightens
as she recognizes LAUREN CHANDLER, a beautiful, fifty
year old, self-possessed woman, walking through
the crowd.

                         ROBIN
                      (waving)
           Mom.
                   (calling louder)
           Mom!

Lauren spots Robin, waves, and hurries toward her.
The women embrace. Robin starts to cry.

                                          (CONTINUED)

                         LAUREN
                    (concerned)
          Baby, baby.
                    (beat)
          What's the matter?

                         ROBIN
                    (controlling herself)
          I...I left Tom.

Lauren looks at her daughter in surprise.

                         LAUREN
          You...?

                         TOM'S VOICE
          Robin...

A look of panic crosses Robin's face. She pulls
away from her mother and runs blindly down the platform.

3.   EXT.   STATELY SUBURBAN HOME   DAY

Lauren and TOM BALLARD, a rugged, handsome man,
slowly walk up the path to the front entrance.

A note on television comedy series scripts: Comedy
series are shot either three-camera film or tape, or
single-camera film. If the program is shot single-camera
film, the standard Teleplay/Screenplay script form may be
used. If the program is shot three-camera, the following
format and model should be followed.

Television comedy series scriptwriting is a demanding
art and an exacting craft. The basic element, as in any
script meant to entertain, is a good story with believable
characters. But, in addition, the writer must pay attention to those limits imposed by the series format and
production realities; i.e., the number and scope of the sets
must be limited (to write a scene where the main problem
occurs in a bowling alley is to invite rejection on budget-
ary grounds; it is advisable to be aware of the series'
permanent, standing, sets), the continuing series characters
must be meaningfully included in the script, and must act
in a manner consistent with their prior actions, etc.

The script form also reflects the requirements of the
thirty-minute time slot. A comedy series script usually
contains two acts and a tag. Each act is comprised of
three scenes running from six to fourteen pages. Act One
presents the problem and the complications and Act Two shows
the attempted solutions and the final resolution. The Tag
generally provides some commentary on the entire premise.
The total length of the script varies between fifty and
sixty pages. Due to the nature of the three-camera technique, camera directions are seldom given.

The Format For Television Comedy Series

1. Camera directions (if used), scene descriptions, and
   stage directions are typed within the margins of
   15 and 55 pica spaces.

2. Dialogue is typed within the margins of 25 and 55 pica
   spaces. The name of the speaking character heads
   (in UPPER CASE) his lines of dialogue. Instructions
   as to how lines are to be delivered (lamely, resigned,
   whispering) are placed in parentheses two lines beneath the character's name and within the same margins
   as the dialogue.

3. Use UPPER CASE for:

   ACT and TAG HEADINGS,
   INT. or EXT., at heading of scene,
   INDICATION OF PLACE, at heading of scene,
   INDICATION OF DAY OR NIGHT, at heading of scene,
   ALL CAMERA DIRECTIONS, SCENE DESCRIPTIONS, and
       STAGE DIRECTIONS,
   NAMES OF CHARACTERS, except when included in dialogue,
   PARENTHETICAL DIRECTION OF HOW LINES ARE TO BE DELIVERED,
   MORE, when used to indicate that a character's
       dialogue is continued on the following page,
   CONT'D, when used to indicate that a character's
       dialogue is continued from a preceding page,
   SCENE TRANSITION DEVICES, when they are specifically
       stated, and
   ACT and SHOW CLOSINGS.

4. Dialogue is written in mixed case, in the usual way.

5. Use single spacing for:

   Camera directions,
   Scene descriptions,
   Stage directions, and
   Sound or effects cues.

6. Use double spacing to separate:

    Transitions from scene headings,
    The first line of scene description or stage directions
        from the scene heading,
    The character name (when heading lines of dialogue) from
        stage directions or scene descriptions,
    The lines of dialogue from the character name which
        heads them,
    The lines of dialogue themselves,
    The dialogue from the character name heading the next
        lines of dialogue,
    The dialogue from the following stage directions or
        scene descriptions,
    The dialogue or description from transitional indicators,
        and
    Transitional devices from act or show closings.

7. Underline:

    Sound cues,
    Character entrances,
    Character exits,
    Act and tag headings, and
    Act and show closings.

ACT ONE

                    (The first page of each scene, ACT TWO,
                    and TAG duplicate the spacing of this
                    page. Scenes are not labelled
                    as such at the top of the page.)

(line 34) FADE IN:

(line 36) INT. OR EXT.   WHERE SCENE IS SET   TIME SCENE IS SET

(line 38) THE CHARACTERS ARE INTRODUCED AND THE
           SCENE IS DESCRIBED WITHIN THE MARGINS OF
           15 AND 55 PICA. THIS LEAVES A LARGE
           WHITE AREA TO THE RIGHT FOR REWRITING
           DURING REHERSALS. IF A CHARACTER ENTERS,
           IT IS INDICATED BY UNDERLINING.

                              CHARACTER'S NAME

                    (THE MANNER IN WHICH THE CHARACTER

                    DELIVERS LINES) The words of

                    dialogue are typed in this

                    manner, within the margins of

                    25 and 55 pica.

                              ANOTHER CHARACTER

                    If the lines of dialogue must extend

                              (MORE)

(Set pica tabs at:)
           15   25   40   55   79

(line 4)

(line 6)   CHARACTER (CONT'D)

        from one page to the next,

        indicate as above.

IF A <u>NOISE OCCURS</u> IT IS UNDERLINE.

                                ANOTHER CHARACTER

        More dialogue.

AND MORE DESCRIPTION, AS WE,

                                        TRANSITION TO:

                        <u>END ACT ONE</u>

        (If the transition is from one scene to
        another, indicate the transition device
        and start a new page with no indication
        that it is the end of the scene.)

(16th line)   IT'S THE LAW

(18th line)   "A Horse of a Different Color"

(21st line)   Written by

                     Robert McKee

(28th line)   SCENE - PAGE

                       A - 1

                       B - 8

                       C - 19

                       D - 33

                       E - 41

                       F - 47

                       G - 56

(51st line)   Represented by:

                                         I.C.M.
                                         8899 Beverly Boulevard
                                         Los Angeles, CA 90048
                                         213-550-4000

O'BRIAN GIVES MAY AN AFFECTIONATE HUG.

                    MAY

          (WISTFULLY) I wish I was going

          with you, but I'd never get on...

                    O'BRIAN

          (INTERRUPTING) You are.

                    MAY

          (CONTINUING)..an airplane?

          (REALIZING WHAT HE HAS SAID, MAY

          BACKS TOWARD THE WALL, TERRIFIED)

          An airplane?

O'BRIAN AND JENNY EACH TAKE ONE OF MAY'S
ARMS AND THEY EXIT UP THE STAIRS.

JUNIOR SHAKES HIS HEAD IN DISBELIEF.

                    JUNIOR

          (TO MAX) Normal?

MAX SHRUGS.

                    MAY

          (O.S.) An airplane?

                              FADE OUT:

              END OF ACT ONE

ACT TWO

FADE IN:

INT. AIRPLANE'S MAIN CABIN DAY

MAY IS IN A FETAL POSITION ON THE SOFA,
HEAD BURIED IN HER HANDS, SHAKING.
O'BRIAN ENTERS, FACE LATHERED, RAZOR IN
HAND. NOTICING MAY, HE CROSSES TO HER.

                    O'BRIAN

          (KINDLY) You can look up now,

          Mrs. Braddock.

                    MAY

          (STILL HIDING) Have we landed?

                    O'BRIAN

          Half an hour ago.

                    MAY

          (SITTING UP AND LOOKING AROUND

          NERVOUSLY) The pilot?

A note about the TV commercial/public service announcement forms: Whether elaborate or simple, produced on film
or tape, the commercial and the PSA are, with one exception,
written in two columns. With only minute variations in the
format between station and station or production house and
production house, the following are universal examples of
the form.

The samples (the shared-ID, the PSA, and the product
commercial) have other commonalities: they identify client
and specify length and often play dates. They are, of
course, persuasive communications, and use direct, personal
address. They are exactingly timed.

The PSA sample represents an announcement written and
distributed to stations by the originating service agency.
It therefore contains more specific identifying and legal
information.

The single exception to a double-column layout of
commercials and PSAs could occur in a simple, minimum-
budget studio production setting. In this case, the
one-column TV dramatic script form might be used, with
the director adding notations and directions in the open
column immediately prior to production.

(TV Shared-ID Sample)

<u>KLM-TV CONTINUITY</u>

CLIENT: TURF, Inc. (sustaining)   DATE: November 6

INSTRUCTIONS: Shared-ID   TO Nov. 13

              LIVE, 10-SECONDS

<u>VIDEO</u>	<u>AUDIO</u>

SLIDE: <u>#4T7</u>
 	
    TURF playground
    with caption
    and Channel 3
    logo.
	ANNCR: San Francisco's youngsters
	need playgrounds like this.
	Support TURF ... Toward
	Unified Recreational
	Facilities.
	KLM-TV, Channel 3, San
	Francisco.

(Public Service Spot, prepared for distribution)

Legal title
and address
of agency
originating
the announce-
ment.

TURF, Inc.
4321 Angel Place
San Francisco 94123

Start Using: Nov. 6

Stop Using: Nov. 13

Identifica-
tion and
telephone
of the con-
tact.

Randolph Grey, Chairman
555/9736

READING TIME -- 20 Seconds

VIDEO	AUDIO
Slide # 5T7	Kids can play in the streets -- it
(Dangerous street with kids scooting between cars, garbage cans.)	might teach survival. But we think there's a better place ...
Slide # 9T7	a well-supervised, superbly-equipped playground. We're working
(Neat, well-equipped TURF playground. Pleased kids in FG.)	to build more places like this for San Francisco's youngsters.
Slide # 7T7	We need your help. Please contact
(Playground with "TURF" caption and phone number.)	TURF -- Toward Unified Recreational Facilities -- TURF, San Francisco.

Slide numbers
have been
filled in by
the station.
Slide descrip-
tions help
announcer
interpret the
copy and assure
quick identifi-
cation.

City Depart-
ment of Social
Services Regis-
tration number.

Social Service Card #420

55

FOOTE, CONE & BELDING/HONIG
2727 W. Sixth Street
Los Angeles, California
BROADCAST DEPARTMENT

CLIENT: MAZDA MOTORS OF AMERICA
PRODUCT: RX3-SP--Rotary Engine
TITLE: "RX3-SP-30"
LENGTH: 30 Seconds
NUMBER: QMCS7050

VIDEO	AUDIO
OPEN ON CAR DRIVING BY CAMERA. SUPER: SEARS POINT RACEWAY.	ANNOUNCER (VO): This is the new Mazda RX3-SP. Rest assured, the SP does not stand for slow poke.
CUT TO CAR DRIVING BY TREE.	
CUT TO TREE LOSING ALL ITS LEAVES.	SFX: (WIND BLOWING AND LEAVES RUSTLING)
CUT TO FRONT VIEW CAR MOVING TOWARD CAMERA.	It's got an air dam up front . . . a remarkable, improved rotary engine . . .
CAR DRIVES BY WATER JUG. CUT TO CLOSEUP OF WATER JUG BREAKING.	SFX: (WATER JUG BREAKING)
CUT TO CAR DRIVING BY CAMERA. CAR DRIVES BY SHED.	independent suspension system . . . semi-monocoque construction . . .
CUT TO SHED COLLAPSING.	SFX: (SHED COLLAPSING)
CUT TO CAR DRIVING BY CAMERA.	and the breeding of over one hundred racing victories in international competition.
CUT TO CLOSEUP OF DRIVER GIVING THUMBS-UP SIGN.	The Mazda RX3-SP . . . it'll make a believer out of you. Fast.
LOGO.	

A note about the one- and two-column TV scripts: Programs to be produced "live onto tape" by means of multiple TV cameras rather than by film techniques may employ either of the following script forms. Scene numbers are not necessary because the progression of recording coincides with that of performance; only a minimal amount of post-production editing may be called for, and the drama's continuity, as well as its substance, will have been recorded.

The two forms are identical in content and would produce identical results. A comparison is instructive: the two-column version is more compact and appears more conventional in layout, but in the actual production situation, many directors prefer the one-column version for its principal virtue--its blank left side accommodates pencilled notations specifying directorially-tailored cuts or dissolves from one camera to another according to the cameras' numbers, camera or subject movements, and music and sound cues with identification of their sources.

(Line 13)   THE CAROLYN BESSON SHOW

(Line 28)   "Sky Command"

(Line 32)   Story and Teleplay
(Line 34)   by
(Line 36)   Zaven Yuralian

(Line 53)   FIRST DRAFT   Zaven Yuralian
               January 1, 1977   1035 North 'H' Street
                                              Fremont, Nebr. 68025

                                              (608) 721-8845

FADE IN ON GENERAL DESCRIPTION OF SCENE --
IN THIS CASE, THE INTERIOR OF A BUSY AIR-
CRAFT HANGER OF PRE-WORLD WAR II VINTAGE.
AFTER DESCRIBING SCENE, THE CAMERA MOVES
IN TO FOCUS ON MAJOR CHARACTER. IN THIS
SCENE, IT IS LON, AN AGING, OVER-BLOWN
MAN OF PRETENSIONS: A GOOD PILOT, THE
COMING WAR MAY PASS HIM BY. HE STANDS,
FRETTING, ALONGSIDE A PARTIALLY-DISMANTLED
ENGINE.

GENERAL BACKGROUND NOISES -- TOOLS, DRILLS,
OCCASIONAL CONVERSATION. IN THE BACK-
GROUND CAN BE HEARD MUSIC IN A VAGUELY
MARTIAL RHYTHM.

SUDDENLY, LON TURNS AND YELLS OFF-CAMERA.

LON (VERY LOUDLY): Hey! Billy! C'mon

over here: move! (LOOKS DEFIANTLY AT

OTHER MECHANICS) I wanna show ya somethin'

... and now!!

MUSIC SUBTLY BECOMES MINOR, OMINOUS.

CAMERA MOVES TO WIDER SHOT AS BILLY, THE
OVER-WORKED HEAD MECHANIC, ENTERS. HE IS
DESCRIBED, AND THE ACTION THEN CONTINUES.

CU BILLY.

BILLY (TIRED): Yes, sir. What can we

do for you? If it's about the super-

chargers ...

MUSIC BUILDS.

MS LON. CAMERA TILTS DOWN TO SHOW HIM
GRAB A SNAKE-LIKE HANDFUL OF WIRES, THEN
THE CAMERA ZOOMS BACK AS HE RAISES THEM
ABOVE HIS HEAD AND RIPS THEM FROM THEIR
DISTRIBUTOR ON THE ENGINE.

<u>SOUND OF WIRES RIPPING, A FEW GASPS,
STIFLED CRIES, AND THEN SILENCE FOR SEV-
ERAL LONG MOMENTS.</u>

CU BILLY: ASTONISHED, FEARFUL. WHEN HE
CAN FIND HIS NERVE, HE SPEAKS.

<u>BILLY (GASPING)</u>: But ... but, that

Pratt-Whitney ... I worked on it all

night ...

CU LON, LIVID WITH ANGER.

<u>LON (ALMOST OUT OF CONTROL, AT THE TOP
OF HIS LUNGS)</u>: The next time, Billy,

m'boy, you do the job <u>right</u>! By God,

(CHOKING WITH RAGE) <u>I've</u> got to take

that crate into the air -- not <u>you</u>!

TWO-SHOT AS LON GRABS THE FRONT OF
BILLY'S COVERALLS WITH LEFT HAND; BIL-
LY OBVIOUSLY AFRAID.

<u>BILLY</u>: But you ... you ... (TRIES TO

GET HIS BREATH) ... you told me to

correct the de-icer. I thought you

wanted to get it ...

BEFORE BILLY CAN COMPLETE HIS SENTENCE,
LON DECKS HIM WITH A RIGHT UPPERCUT, THE
CAMERA MOVING IN TO CATCH THE PUNCH AS
IT LANDS, AND THEN TO FOLLOW BILLY AS HE
SLUMPS TO THE FLOOR.

SOUND OF SLAMMING FIST. GASPS OF ON-
LOOKERS.

SNEAK IN MARTIAL MUSIC AGAIN, B.G.

CU LON, SMILING.

LON (FEELING BETTER, ALMOST HAPPY):

Well, happy landings, Billy. You jerk!

MUSIC UP FULL.

COVER SHOT OF HANGER, THE MECHANICS TURN-
ING TOWARD LON IN DISBELIEF AS HE EXITS
TRIUMPHANTLY. CAMERA SLOWLY MOVES IN TO-
WARD BILLY, BUT BEFORE IT CAN REACH A
CLOSEUP OF HIM, FADE TO BLACK.

FADE SOUND OUT.

(Set pica tabs at:)
40   75

61

VIDEO	AUDIO
FADE IN ON GENERAL DESCRIPTION OF SCENE -- IN THIS CASE THE INTERIOR OF A BUSY AIRCRAFT HANGER OF PRE-WORLD WAR II VINTAGE. AFTER DESCRIBING SCENE, THE CAMERA MOVES IN TO FOCUS ON MAJOR CHARACTER. IN THIS SCENE IT IS LON, AN AGING, OVER-BLOWN MAN OF PRETENSIONS: A GOOD PILOT, THE COMING WAR MAY PASS HIM BY. HE FRETS ALONGSIDE A PARTIALLY-DISMANTLED ENGINE.	GENERAL BACKGROUND NOISES -- TOOLS, DRILLS, OCCASIONAL CONVERSATION. IN THE BACKGROUND CAN BE HEARD MUSIC IN A VAGUELY MARTIAL RHYTHM.
SUDDENLY, LON TURNS AND YELLS OFF-CAMERA.	LON (VERY LOUDLY): Hey! Billy! C'mon over here: move! (LOOKS DEFIANTLY AT OTHER MECHANICS) I wanna show ya somethin' ... and now!! MUSIC SUBTLY BECOMES MINOR, OMINOUS.
CAMERA MOVES TO WIDER SHOT AS BILLY, THE OVER-WORKED HEAD MECHANIC, ENTERS. HE IS DESCRIBED, AND THE ACTION THEN CONTINUES. CU BILLY.	BILLY (TIRED): Yes, sir. What can we do for you? If it's about the super-chargers ... MUSIC BUILDS

62

MS LON. CAMERA TILTS DOWN TO
SHOW HIM GRAB A SNAKE-LIKE
HANDFUL OF WIRES, THEN THE
CAMERA ZOOMS BACK AS HE RAIS-
ES THEM ABOVE HIS HEAD AND
RIPS THEM FROM THEIR DISTRIB-
UTOR ON THE ENGINE.

SOUND OF WIRES RIPPING, A FEW
GASPS, STIFLED CRIES, AND THEN
SILENCE FOR SEVERAL LONG MOMENTS.

CU BILLY: ASTONISHED, FEAR-
FUL. WHEN HE CAN FIND HIS
NERVE, HE SPEAKS.

BILLY (GASPING): But ... but,
that Pratt-Whitney ... I worked
on it all night ...

CU LON, LIVID WITH ANGER.

LON (ALMOST OUT OF CONTROL, AT
THE TOP OF HIS LUNGS): The next
time, Billy, m'boy, you do the
job right! By God, (CHOKING
WITH RAGE) I've got to take that
crate into the air -- not you!

TWO-SHOT AS LON GRABS THE
FRONT OF BILLY'S COVERALLS
WITH LEFT HAND; BILLY OBVIOUS-
LY AFRAID.

BILLY: But you ... you ... (TRIES
TO GET HIS BREATH) ... you told
me to correct the de-icer. I
thought you wanted to get it ...

BEFORE BILLY CAN COMPLETE HIS
SENTENCE, LON DECKS HIM WITH
A RIGHT UPPERCUT, THE CAMERA
MOVING IN TO CATCH THE PUNCH
AS IT LANDS, AND THEN TO FOL-
LOW BILLY AS HE SLUMPS TO THE
FLOOR.

SOUND OF SLAMMING FIST. GASPS
OF ON-LOOKERS.

SNEAK IN MARTIAL MUSIC AGAIN, B.G.

CU LON, SMILING.

LON (FEELING BETTER, ALMOST HAP-PY): Well, happy landings, Billy.

You jerk!

COVER SHOT OF HANGER, THE MECHANICS TURNING TOWARD LON IN DISBELIEF AS HE EXITS TRIUMPHANTLY. CAMERA SLOW-LY MOVES IN TOWARD BILLY, BUT BEFORE IT CAN REACH A CLOSEUP OF HIM, FADE TO BLACK.

MUSIC UP FULL.

FADE SOUND OUT.

(Set pica tabs at:)

14   40   46   75

64

<u>A note about the radio drama/documentary production
script</u>: Although such productions are rarely created
today, the script form itself remains standard and has
application in the broadly-practiced radio "production"
commercial, as well as in such purely aural presentations
as audio recordings. Wherever it is necessary to use
compound production elements (sound effects, music,
dialogue), as contrasted with straight narration, this
form is called for.

The Format For Radio Production Scripts

1. Script content is typed across the page so as to allow
   for approximately 1-inch left and 1-1/4-inch right
   margins.

2. Dialogue occupies a column between 28 and 72 pica spaces.
   Name of the speaking character (in UPPER CASE) is in
   line with and to the left of his first line. Instructions as to how lines should be spoken (if necessary)
   appear in parentheses and UPPER CASE immediately to
   the right of his or her name, preceding the line
   itself. Dialogue is typed in regular upper and lower
   case letters.

3. Lines of dialogue, music cues, and sound effects cues are
   numbered along the left margin of the page at 10 pica
   spaces; they are numbered consecutively throughout the
   entire script.

4. Music and sound effects cues and descriptions commence
   at 21 pica spaces.

5. Use underlining for all music and sound effects cues.

6. Use parentheses to enclose:

   Any material inserted into a line which is not part
     of the line itself (directions for reading the line,
     music, and sound effects notations), and
   Descriptions of music wherever they occur.

7. Use double spacing throughout the script; single spacing
   is not used in radio scripts.

8. Use UPPER CASE for:

   All UNSPOKEN INSTRUCTIONS within a line of dialogue,
   All MUSIC CUES,
   All SOUND EFFECTS CUES, and
   NAMES OF CHARACTERS, except where these are to be
     spoken.

9. Words are not broken at the end of a line and continued
   on the following line (although hyphenated words may
   be).

10. Lines should not be broken at the bottom of a page and
    carried over to the following page; whever possible,
    a new cue should commence a new page.

13   MAN: Speaks here. (THEN, MORE SOFTLY) He speaks
                        once more.

14   WOMAN: Answers. As she elaborates, her lines don't
                        tend to go beyond the margins set at right.

15   MAN: Responds, until he completes his dramatic tag.

16   (MUSIC: WHAT IT DOES OR WHAT ITS MOOD IS - WHAT IT
                        THEN DOES - AND, FINALLY, HOW IT IS DISPOSED
                        OF.)

17   WOMAN: She continues to relate her story here, until
                        she is interrupted by ...

18   SOUND: INDENTED, AS IS MUSIC, A SOUND CUE STATES
                        FIRST ITS IDENTIFICATION, THEN ITS QUALITY,
                        AND THEN ITS PERSPECTIVE, AND FINALLY THE WAY
                        IT IS TERMINATED.

19   WOMAN: Reacts to the sound here, as matters progress.

67

(Set pica tabs at:)
11   18   24   30   78

107	REINISH:	Nearly a third of the world already! My God, <u>wiped</u> <u>out</u>! In just three weeks. Three weeks since <u>we</u> created Virus "13" -- but we can't give up, Berns. There has to be a way!
108	BERNS:	<u>If</u> there is, we alone can find it. You and I are the only ones who know anything about Virus "13". If we can't, the whole world ... (BITTERLY) We were going to aid mankind -- we were offering humanity a medical improvement undreamed of.
109		<u>SOUND: DOOR OPENS, OFF.</u>
110	REINISH:	Where are you going?
111	BERNS:	(OFF MIKE) To the hospital again. Maybe they have some new information about the early symptoms. I'll be back early tomorrow, Doctor.
112		<u>SOUND: DOOR CLOSES.</u>
113		<u>(MUSIC: SEARCHING MOTIF ... BRING IN LOW ... BUILD IN TEMPO ... THEN SEGUE TO:)</u>
114		<u>SOUND: INSISTENT KNOCK ON DOOR ... DOOR OPENS.</u>
115	BERNS:	(FADE ON MIKE ... EXCITED ... BARGES IN) Reynolds! Reynolds, where's Dr. Reinish? I think I've got the answer! Maybe Reinish and I can work it out -- we'll have to work it out <u>together</u>, he and I -- but at least the world has a chance! (STOPS SHORT) Well, Reynolds?
116	REYNOLDS:	Doctor, there's ... there's been a ... I ...

68

117   BERNS: What? What's wrong? Where's Reinish?

118   REYNOLDS: I thought you heard. (PAUSE ... THEN DAZED)

             Dr. Reinish died last night -- Virus "13".

119   (MUSIC: STAB ... UP FOR CRESCENDO ... HOLD FOR

             DRAMATIC TAG.)

(Radio Dialogue Commercial Sample)

ANNCR: Pardon me, ma'm, but I see you're buying America's leading hair-care. Woncka's -- W-O-N-C-K-A-S -- Woncka's.

LADY: Woncka's hair-care is marvelous.

ANNCR: Why do you insist on Woncka's?

LADY: I just love Woncka's hair-care. In fact, the whole family loves the new me, thanks to Woncka's.

ANNCR: Why Woncka's?

LADY: Especially my husband.

ANNCR: But why Woncka's?

LADY: It's so easy ... I just follow the instructions...

ANNCR: Why Woncka's?

LADY: Just empty the gold packet, add warm water, and then apply ...

ANNCR: But why ...?

LADY: The girls at the club love the easy way it applies, the color and life it ...

ANNCR: But, lady, why Woncka's?

LADY: Why? Why not Woncka's?!

<u>KLMN RADIO CONTINUITY</u>

CLIENT: DANSK INTERIORS   DATE: DEC. 7, 1977

INSTRUCTIONS: "THE NOT-A-COMMERCIAL"

               LIVE

NO ONE -- NOT EVEN ONE OF THE DANSK (<u>DON</u>-SK) INTERIORS EX-PERTS -- WOULD LIKE TO BE ACCUSED OF INVENTING THE NON-COMMERCIAL, <u>BUT</u> DANSK INTERIORS HAS JUST CONCLUDED A VERY SUCCESSFUL ONCE-A-YEAR SALE ... AND, WELL, THINGS ARE IN A MESS ... AND THAT'S NOT LIKE THEM. AS UP-TO-DATE SAN DIEGANS KNOW -- AND DANSK IS PROUD TO ADMIT -- DANSK ALWAYS WAS A SHOWCASE FOR THE FINEST MODERN FURNISHINGS AND ACCESSORIES .... BUT AFTER A VERY BUSY SALE WEEKEND ... DANSK NEEDS SOME TIME TO RELAX. AS ANOTHER YEAR BETWEEN SALES BEGINS, THEY'D LIKE TO POINT TO THE FACT THAT TRUE VALUE IS SOMETHING YOU DON'T PUT ON SALE ... AT DANSK INTERIORS, THERE'S PERENNIAL VALUE AS YOU'LL SEE WHEN THE NEW MERCHANDISE IS PUT ON DISPLAY. VISIT DANSK INTERIORS IN EL CAJON'S NEW LA PAZ CENTER ... BUT GIVE THEM A COUPLE OF DAYS TO STRAIGHTEN THINGS UP. THERE, NOW ... THAT WASN'T A COMMERCIAL, WAS IT?

PART II

Writers' Aids

A note about storyboards: A pictorial medium, the storyboard provides a fine communication tool, a link between written words and ultimate visual motion. It should not be thought of as useful only to TV commercial work, because its value extends into all areas of motion pictures. Some are more finished than others; they may be crude "roughs," merely sketches, or they may be in full color and fastidiously detailed, with a frame for every few seconds of screen time. Nearly all will have a frame for each shot; all will represent the lens' view (they will not appear as floor plans or include material outside the lens' framing); and they will indicate correlations between sounds and visuals as these occur.

TELEVISION COMMERCIAL

FILM ANIMATION, 30 Seconds

CLIENT: STEINMAN CHEMICAL CO.
PRODUCT: Sure-Stop Pellets
TITLE: "Rodents, Cute & Not So"

FADE IN on:

1. Forest floor with activity of cute small animals.

Music:
(Something twittery.)

Announcer:
Little animals can be cute ... furry folk of the forest ... cuddly creatures of books we knew as children, long remembered.

2. Closer shot; one animal washes himself, while another blinks charmingly.

3. An "indoor" mouse, sweeping her livingroom.

Even the humble, bustling mouse.

HARD CUT to:

4. Lean, tattered, bristling rat. He is soiled, venomous.

Music:
(A discord!)

Announcer:
But never this! Who of us can imagine this

SUPERIMPOSE:

4x. The railing of a child's crib, in which baby lies asleep. The rat is now on this railing.

near our sleeping child?

5. Close shot on sleeping baby.

That's why at Steinman Chemical, we've done something about it.

DISSOLVE to:

Music:
(Placid, with a hint of the triumphant.)

6. Laboratory paraphernalia; growing into closeup from it is a can of Sure-Stop.

The can of Sure-Stop is held in position as the background

Announcer:
Steinman Sure-Stop Pellets declare your home off-limits to rodents -- permanently.

DISSOLVES to:

Steinman Sure-Stop: safe for your pets and you --

6x. A cozy home interior.

the end for household rodents!

FADE OUT.

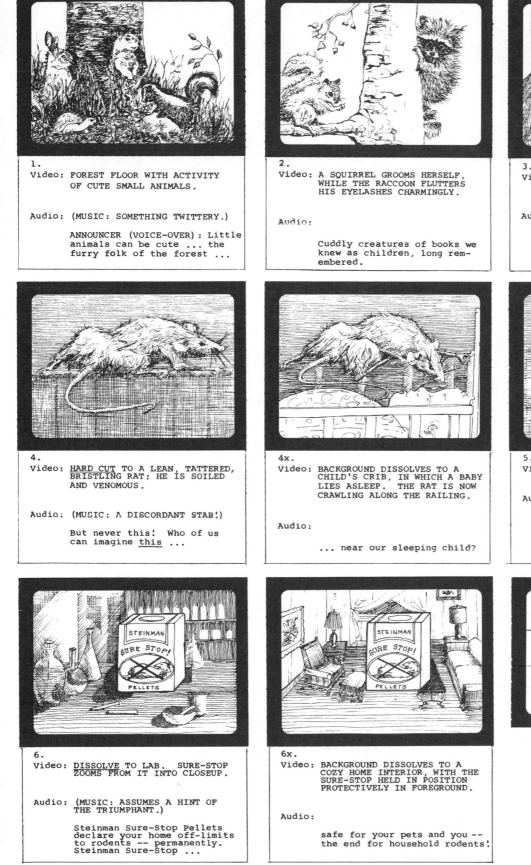

1.
Video: FOREST FLOOR WITH ACTIVITY OF CUTE SMALL ANIMALS.

Audio: (MUSIC: SOMETHING TWITTERY.)

ANNOUNCER (VOICE-OVER): Little animals can be cute ... the furry folk of the forest ...

2.
Video: A SQUIRREL GROOMS HERSELF, WHILE THE RACCOON FLUTTERS HIS EYELASHES CHARMINGLY.

Audio:

Cuddly creatures of books we knew as children, long remembered.

3.
Video: AN "INDOOR MOUSE" TIDIES HER LIVINGROOM.

Audio:

Even the humble, bustling mouse.

4.
Video: HARD CUT TO A LEAN, TATTERED, BRISTLING RAT; HE IS SOILED AND VENOMOUS.

Audio: (MUSIC: A DISCORDANT STAB!)

But never this! Who of us can imagine this ...

4x.
Video: BACKGROUND DISSOLVES TO A CHILD'S CRIB, IN WHICH A BABY LIES ASLEEP. THE RAT IS NOW CRAWLING ALONG THE RAILING.

Audio:

... near our sleeping child?

5.
Video: SLEEPING BABY.

Audio: (MUSIC: QUIET, ALMOST PLACID.)

That's why at Steinman Chemical, we've done something about it.

6.
Video: DISSOLVE TO LAB. SURE-STOP ZOOMS FROM IT INTO CLOSEUP.

Audio: (MUSIC: ASSUMES A HINT OF THE TRIUMPHANT.)

Steinman Sure-Stop Pellets declare your home off-limits to rodents -- permanently. Steinman Sure-Stop ...

6x.
Video: BACKGROUND DISSOLVES TO A COZY HOME INTERIOR, WITH THE SURE-STOP HELD IN POSITION PROTECTIVELY IN FOREGROUND.

Audio:

safe for your pets and you -- the end for household rodents!

Client:	Product:
Steinman Chemical Group	Sure-Stop Rodent Pellets

Length:	Description:	Page:
:30	"Rodents Cute and Otherwise"	1 of 1

Date:	Commercial #:	Client Approval:
4/17/77	4	S. Lubin

TIMING TIPS

With experience, media writers gain a sense of playing-time per given amount of commercial copy, dialogue, or dramatic action. Until that experience is gained, it is helpful to have some generalized "rules of thumb" for the translation of words and action descriptions into consumed time.

Several variables prevent exact word/time equivalencies: The script format used (for instance, the one-column TV script form calls for a 50% increase in number of pages beyond that required for the teleplay/screenplay script format; the two-column TV script form calls for 20% less than the one-column version); the balance of spoken words and action (spoken words usually take less time than "silent" actions); and the intention and style of the spoken words both in announce copy and in dramatic forms (it takes the same amount of time to say "Pestilence, hunger, the mourning of a nation lost," as it does to say, "You'll want to get down to Fenstermacher's right away for this sensational give-away sale!").

Noting those variables, the following timing guides suffice:

WORDS	EQUAL	SECONDS
18		8
44		20
61		28
130		60

WORDS	PICA MARGIN SET	LINES
30	AT 15 AND 75	3
50		5
70		7
310	("monologue" only)	1 page

OUTLINE PAGES	TELEPLAY/SCREENPLAY	TIMING
10-15		1/2 hour
15-25		1 hour
25-40		1-1/2 hour
40-60	FEATURE FILM	2 hours

SCRIPT PAGES	TELEPLAY/SCREENPLAY	TIMING
1		52 seconds
3		2-1/2 mins.
7		6 minutes
30		1/2 hour
60		1 hour
128	FEATURE FILM	2 hours

Finally, the timing of lines or pages is most accurately arrived at by reading them _aloud_, and in the delivery style wanted, to a clock's second hand. It is always a good idea to write a few words shorter than the time indicated. Where production elements occur (bits of business, sound effects, music bridges, etc.) these should be imagined closely, and the reading paced accordingly.

PROTECTING THE PROPERTY: COPYRIGHT AND REGISTRATION

If you have followed the appropriate script model as sug-
gested in this booklet, have typed your script using a pica
typewriter on good quality 8-1/2 by 11 inch white paper (avoid
the "erasable" types or copy paper), have proofread the
original and corrected all spelling and grammatical errors,
have made several copies of the script and stored the original
in a safe place, have three-hole punched the copies and put
them into plain but sturdy covers, you are ready to protect
the contents of your script by establishing a completion date
before sending it on to agents and producers.

The only method of establishing a completion date and
securing statutory protection for your property is by copyrighting it, an action which now confers protection of it for
the lifetime of the copyright holder plus fifty years. Under
the Copyright Act of 1976, "all original works of authorship
can be registered for copyright regardless of whether they are
published or unpublished" with the exceptions of ideas, outlines,
treatments, and titles--none of which are copyrightable. In
order to be fully protected under the new law, notice of copyright must "be placed on all publicly distributed copies." This
notice consists of the placement of the symbol ©, or the word
"Copyright," or its abbreviation "Copr.," followed by the year
of first publication or distribution, and ending with the name
of the copyright holder. The notice should appear on the title
page, the page immediately following, or any other conspicuous
place "permanently legible to an ordinary user of the work."
If this notice is omitted and the work is not registered within
five years of publication, the property goes into the public
domain. However, the work may be registered within three months
of first publication or distribution with no loss of rights.

The first step in copyright registration is to request the
proper form from the Information and Publications Section,
Copyright Office, Library of Congress, Washington, D.C. 20559.
Form TX should be requested for nondramatic fiction or non-
fiction, and for advertising copy. Form PA designates works
of the performing arts (play scripts in whatever medium, and
other dramatized work); VA deals with visual arts creations
(e.g.: storyboards); SR covers sound recordings. If a work
falls into more than one class (e.g.: a TV commercial containing a score for a musical jingle, or a storyboard with
narration cast in poetry), a single registration in any
appropriate class will protect all of the work's copyrightable
material. The completed form, one copy of an unpublished work
(two copies are needed if the work is published), and a check
for $10.00 made payable to Register of Copyrights should be
sent to: Register of Copyrights, Library of Congress,
Washington, D.C. 20559, via first-class mail.

Because the old copyright laws provided only common law protection for unpublished works, many media writers did not bother to copyright. Instead, they registered their scripts with the Writers Guild of America (WGA), a labor organization representing screen, television and radio writers. It is comprised of the Writers Guild of America, East, with offices at 22 West 48th Street, New York, New York 10036, and the Writers Guild of America, West, headquartered at 8955 Beverly Boulevard, Los Angeles, California 90048.

The WGA negotiates basic agreements in screen, television, and radio regarding working conditions, payment scales, credits, residuals, agency representation and the like. It does not obtain employment for writers, offer writing instruction, or submit material to producers. The minimum requirements for Guild membership is "that you have had employment as a writer for screen, television, or radio or that you have sold original material to one of these media. The initiation fee is $400.00."

As a service to its members, and to aspiring writers who are not yet members, the WGA has a Manuscript Registration Service. Unlike copyrighting, this service does not confer statutory protection. It does, however, provide evidence of the writer's claimed authorship of the property involved and of the date of its completion. To register a script one sends a xeroxed copy on 8-1/2 by 11 inch white or buff paper, typed on one side only, to the Writers Guild of America, West, 8955 Beverly Boulevard, Los Angeles, California 90048, Attention: Manuscript Registration Service. Nonmembers must include a check or money order for $10.00. The script must be registered under the author's full legal name. The Guild will also register formats, treatments, or general descriptions of films, radio and television programs.

Some writers send a copy of the completed script to themselves via Registered Mail. They leave the envelope unopened with the seal intact. This is the least concrete method of determining a completion date in any legal action and is not encouraged.

Neither WGA registration nor copyright proceedings protects titles. The Motion Picture Association, an organization of distributors and producers of feature-length films, administers a title registration service. For an annual subscription fee of $150.00 and the payment of a $150.00 service fee, a nonmember may register a group of ten motion picture titles. While this confers no statutory protection, major producers and distributors are signatories to an agreement recognizing this title registration. For further information contact the Head of Title Registration, Motion Picture Association, 522 Fifth Avenue, New York, New York 10036.

AGENTS

Few motion picture or television producers will read an unsolicited manuscript from an unknown writer. The principal reason for this is that they do not wish to become involved in entangling and time-consuming lawsuits resulting from reading a property which has come to them from a volunteered source. It is important, therefore, for the writer to acquire representation.

The Writers Guild of America, West, Inc., 8955 Beverly Boulevard, Los Angeles, California 90048 (telephone, 213/550-1000), has published a listing of literary and theatrical agencies who subscribe to its Artists' Managers Basic Agreement of 1975. As part of this list, the Guild indicates those agencies who will consider material from novice writers.

A writer should send a letter to one or more of these agencies detailing his professional or academic credentials and briefly describing the nature of the property to be submitted. The agency will indicate whether it is interested in receiving the material for evaluation. This is one of the few ways for a beginner with no industry contacts to get a property read by a professional.

After a period of three to nine weeks, some word will be received from the agency. This may be a polite refusal to represent the script, a "pass" on the specific script but an invitation to submit other properties, a detailed evaluation of the writer's strengths and weaknesses, or an indication of willingness to offer the script to potential buyers.

After representation is agreed upon, the agency will submit the script to the major studios, producers and directors. These submissions may require the duplication of as many as fifty copies of the screenplay and the writer must be prepared to absorb this cost as well as the cost of a professional script typing service.

Then, the writer waits again. The amount of time for any word to be received on the submissions will vary from between three days to a year. It is a game of patience and perseverance. But the writer cannot wait for the first check to arrive; instead, he returns to the typewriter and begins work on the next project.

The process of acquiring an agent and selling a script is long, involved, and frustrating. Successes are few and far between, but they generally come to those who have talent, who are well-prepared, who understand the marketplace, who are sensitively represented, and who have faith in themselves and in their material.

SUGGESTIONS FROM THE PROFESSIONALS

In talking about scripts at a recent Filmex Conference on screenwriting, a panel of producers (Tony Bill, Don Devlin, Harry Gittes, Michael Douglas, Rob Cohen, Steve Tisch and Tamara Asseyev) had these suggestions: that a script not be put into a fancy cover; that a script not include a cast of characters after the title page; that a synopsis of the story not be included after the title page; that a script not be written in any format which includes overly specific, technical information or camera angles; that a script be confined to 130 pages (some of the producers disagreed, commenting that longer works sometimes were acceptable); that a script not include notes apologizing for misspelled words or indicating that any other polish is needed; and, finally, that title pages not indicate that a script has been registered with the Writers' Guild of America. There was some discussion on this final point with the producers agreeing that the script should be protected in some way, but that the prominent display of the registration number was a sign of a neophyte.

READINGS FOR WRITERS

BOOKS:

Anatomy of Criticism, N. Frye, Princeton University Press.

Anatomy of Local Radio-TV Copy, W. Peck, Tab Books.

Aristotle's Poetics, with Commentaries, Golden and Hardison, Prentice-Hall.

Breaking Through, Selling Out, Dropping Dead, W. Bayer, Macmillan.

The Cool Fire, R. Shanks, Norton.

Documentary Film, P. Rotha, Faber & Faber, Ltd.

Dramatic Construction, E. Mabley, Chilton.

Educational Films, L. Herman, Crown.

Elements of Style, Strunk and White, Macmillan.

Fiction Into Film, R. Maddux, et al., Delta.

Film and/as Literature, J. Harrington, Prentice-Hall.

Film Form and the Film Sense, S. Eisenstein, Meridian.

Film Scriptwriting, D. Swain, Hastings House.

Film Techniques and Film Acting, V. Pudovkin, Grove Press.

Hollywood Now, W. Fadiman, Liveright.

The Impact of Film, R. Madsen, Macmillan.

Life of the Drama, E. Bentley, Athenium.

Literature and Film, R. Richardson, Indiana University Press.

Making Movies: From Script to Screen, L. Bobker, Harcourt, Brace, Jovanovich.

The Moving Image, R. Gessner, Dutton.

The Nature of Narrative, Scholes and Kellog, Oxford.

Novels Into Film, G. Bluestone, University of California
    Press.

A Practical Manual of Screen Playwriting for Theatre and
    Television Films, L. Herman, Meridian.

Professional Broadcast Writer's Handbook, S. Field, Tab
    Books.

The Screenwriter Looks at the Screenwriter, W. Froug,
    Delta.

Short Story, Short Film, F. Marcus, Prentice-Hall.

Six-Guns and Society, W. Wright, University of California
    Press.

Talking Pictures: Screenwriters in the American Cinema,
    R. Corliss, Penguin.

The Technique of Screenplay Writing, E. Vale, Grosset &
    Dunlap.

Teleplay; an Introduction to Television Writing, C. Trap-
    nell, Chandler Publishing.

The Television Commercial, Book and Cary, Decker Communica-
    tions, Inc.

The Television Copy Writer, C. Wainright, Hastings House.

The Television Writer, E. Barnouw, Hill & Wang.

Theory and Technique of Playwriting and Screenwriting,
    J. H. Lawson, Putnam & Sons.

The Trouble With Tribbles, D. Gerrold, Ballantine.

The Writer and the Screen, W. Rilla, W. H. Allen.

Writing for Television and Radio (3rd Edition), R. Hilliard,
    Hastings House.

Writing Television and Radio Programs, E. Willis, Holt &
    Rinehart.

PERIODICALS:

"Daily Variety": a trade journal containing information
        about current and pending film and television pro-
        ductions in the United States, as well as articles
        of general interest about the film, TV, music and
        entertainment industries. Highly recommended. A
        subscription is $40.00 per year, from 1400 No.
        Cahuenga Blvd., Hollywood, Calif. 90028.

"The Hollywood Reporter": similar to "Daily Variety" and
        also highly recommended. This trade paper is avail-
        able by subscription for $40.00 per year from P. O.
        Box 1431, Hollywood, Calif. 90028.

"Ross Reports": available for $7.50 for a six-month sub-
        scription from Ross Reports Television, Television
        Index, Inc., 150 Fifth Ave., New York, New York 10011.
        This monthly lists agencies, script contacts for all
        TV series, TV commercial producers, packagers, etc.
        Useful for breakdowns of network programs. This
        directory summarizes programs, cites whether the
        program is taped or filmed, and whether scripts are
        assigned or are accepted on a free-lance basis.

"The Scriptwriter": a new monthly magazine which hopes to
        become the "market survey, craft guide, and forum for
        professional writers of film and television scripts."
        The first two issues contained good articles on the
        writer-agent relationship, marketing trends, Hollywood
        story departments, etc. Available for $25.00 a year
        or $16.00 for six months from P. O. Box 1941, Hollywood,
        Calif. 90028.

"Weekly Variety": a summary of the entertainment industry,
        by the publishers of "Daily Variety." Often presents
        "special issues" dealing with such subjects as inter-
        national broadcasting, world cinema markets, etc. May
        usually be found in libraries, or by subscription at
        $30.00 per year from 1400 No. Cahuenga Blvd., Holly-
        wood, Calif. 90028.

"Writer's Digest": a monthly magazine featuring items of
        all kinds pertaining to the commercial aspects of the
        craft. Although the emphasis is on literary writing,
        there are frequent articles and tips of value to the
        media writer. At $12.00 per year, it is available
        from 9933 Alliance Road, Cincinnati, Ohio 45242.

"The Writer's Market": an annual of limited value to the
     media writer, but occasionally contains such items
     as educational film markets. (Note the following
     entry.)

"The Writer's Yearbook": an annual publication, this is
     an updated supplement to "The Writer's Market" and
     is of some help in specifying market availabilities.
     Most libraries subscribe to both the "Yearbook" and
     the "Market"; where this is not the case, the "Year-
     book" may be obtained for $1.50 and the "Market" for
     $13.50 from 9933 Alliance Road, Cincinnati, Ohio
     45242.

GLOSSARY

Accelerated motion. (see Fast motion).

Act. a major dramatic division, definitive unit of dramatic development in a teleplay (and in motion pictures, except that here the divisions are implicit and the plot proceeds without interruption). In TV, it is usually separated from a similar unit by a commercial "break" or at least by a fade out followed by a fade in.

Action. (1) the patterned movement of a character or an object. (2) In cinema, the term for anything to be seen. (3) In a two-column script format for film, the term heads the column describing the visuals; for TV, the visual column is headed "video."

Adaptation. transposition of a work originally created for one medium into another medium.

Aerial shot. a shot made from overhead by means of a plane, helicopter or crane (see also Crane shot).

Aleatory filming. (1) the cameraman not planning his images in advance, but composing on the spot. (2) Broadly, techniques based upon chance conditions and probability.

Angle. or "angle of view" (see Camera angle).

Animation. (1) bringing to apparent life otherwise inanimate objects or artwork. Successive still drawings, each differing very slightly from one another, will appear to be in motion when filmed in single-frame exposures as will dimensional objects when moved slightly between single exposures. (2) When applied to humans, models, stringless puppets, and similar subjects, the term pixilation is used.

Another angle. an indication of the same or continuing action, but from a different placement of the camera.

Antagonist. the force (embodied in a character, object, or represented by a condition) which threatens the attainment of the goal of the protagonist (to whom the audience gives its allegiance). (See Protagonist.)

Anticlimax. an unintentional letdown in tension following the drama's climax resulting from the tacking on of less consequential material.

Approach. (1) camera movement from a long shot toward a closeup. (2) As an editing term, the conventional method of cutting from long shot (general orientation to the scene) to medium shot (singling out of a specific area of the scene) to closeup (revelation of some detail).

Arc. dolly or truck shot transcribing a curve.

Asynchronous sound. nonsynchronized sound; sound acting in counterpoint to the visuals, rather than as a literal counterpart of them. (E.g., in *The 39 Steps,* a woman screams, but we hear the shriek of a passing train.)

Background. (1) portion of the scene farthest from the camera. (2) Scenery or ground against which drawings (cels) are filmed. (3) Sounds, usually unintelligible or at least secondary, accompanying principal sounds. (Abbreviated BG.)

Back projection. (see Process screen).

Beat. a short, predetermined pause in action or speech.

BG. (see Background).

Billboard. credits at opening (and/or sometimes the closing) of a program listing sponsor, talent, producer, and similar credits.

Board fade. control of all sound through a single master channel (see Fade).

Business. action used to develop or intensify characterization, a plot detail, etc.

Busy. distracting overabundance of inessential visual or aural detail.

Camera angle. the camera's point of view toward the subject: from above ("high angle"), below ("low angle"), or off-axis. The term angle of view is usually used to indicate the angle subtended by the lens (such as wide angle, telephoto, etc.) and so has to do with the subject's size in relation to the frame. (See also Another angle.)

Characterization. the total of behavioral and appearance details which define and give individuality to a person in a radio or screen presentation.

Cinéma-vérité. (1) the use of light-weight, usually hand-held (and consequently flexible and unobtrusive) equipment in documentary filming in order to produce "cinema truth." (2) A series of techniques designed to interfere with or intrude upon the "actuality" before the camera as little as possible.

Climax. high point; tension peak; particularly, as a part of dramatic structure, that place in the action beyond which there can be no further complication or heightening of tension or conflict;

so, the moment at which the protagonist achieves what he has strived for or is defeated. (Often, this term is mistaken for "crisis.") The climax is the action embodiment (not a verbal statement) of the drama's theme.

Closeup. a shot which shows a detail of a subject; most commonly, a shot of the face only, although closeups of eyes or the mouth may be specified. The concept of the closeup is that it eliminates all other aspects of the subject and its background. Its exclusivity and insistence make it a visual exclamation mark. (Abbreviated CU; see also ECU.)

Complication. An unexpected dramatic development which confronts the protagonist, threatening the attainment of his goal.

Conflict. the stuff of all dramatic action and of drama itself: the grappling of forces which seek mutually incompatible objectives.

Confrontation. the bringing together of opposing forces in a pattern of goal definition/conflict/ disastrous result (posing, in turn, further dangers and frustrations of the protagonist's desires).

Cover shot. (see ELS and Establishing shot).

Crane shot. moving shot made from a crane, a large, self-elevating machine on wheels which can swing the camera and its operator through three dimensions as well as move closer toward or farther from the subject.

Credit. display or announcement of person responsible for the creation of, performance in, or other contribution to a program in whatever medium.

Crisis. an event creating suspense; particularly, as a part of dramatic structure, that place in each sequence where the protagonist is thwarted in his reach toward his goal and must try again to achieve it. There are, therefore, many crises within and making up the main body of the drama. Forming the dramatic pattern itself, they rise in intensity until the climax.

Crosscut. to alternate between shots or actions occurring in different locations, usually at the same time, and having some kind of bearing upon one another.

Cross-fade. once a synonym for "dissolve" in film, but currently refers to sound, in which one sound flows into another and ultimately replaces it (see Segue).

CU. (see Closeup).

Cue. (1) an action, word or sound which signals the commencement of another speech or action. (2) Any signal which directs the beginning of a sound or an action segment.

Cut. (1) termination of an image or sound in prep-aration for the presentation of a new image or sound. (2) In film or TV, a conventional, instantaneous transition not achieved by optical effects.

Cut-away. (1) strictly, a shot within a sequence which contains no visual elements from the preceding shot in that sequence. (2) A shot away from the main action.

Deep focus. image sharpness in objects far from as well as close to the camera, thus not emphasizing one spatial plane more than any other. Opposite of shallow focus.

Denouement. the "unravelling"; in dramatic structure, the brief closing section which "ties up loose ends" by explaining some action or situation which had gone before, or which makes disposition of characters. It therefore comes after the obligatory scene and the climax and is not mandatory in good drama because these two high points should themselves "explain" or resolve questions inherent in the conflict.

Deus ex machina. "God in a machine": the convenient but implausible extrication of the protagonist from a hopeless sitation by the transparent manipulation of the author, rather than by qualities of the protagonist's character or the inevitabilities dictated by the circumstances and direction of the plot.

Dialogue. expository conversation between two or more performers. (Note this entry under Sound—speech.)

Dissolve. (1) a fade out superimposed upon a fade in. (2) An optical effect creating a transition from one scene to another by such gradual displacement through overlapping. The connotation of the dissolve is that a change of place and a minor change of time are occurring. It is often likened to a scene curtain (rather than an act curtain) in theatre, as regards time/place change (see Lap dissolve). (3) The aural equivalent is cross-fade, a term also frequently used in cinema lab work.

Dolly shot. a moving shot made by a camera mounted on a dolly, a small, flat, wheeled platform. Usually, such a shot advances directly toward a static subject ("dolly in"), or recedes directly from it ("dolly out"). If the subject is in motion in the same direction as the camera, the term follow shot is used; if the camera advances or recedes at an angle to or parallel to the action, the term tracking shot is used.

Double exposure. (see Multiple exposure).

Down. to visually darken in tonal values, or to diminish in aural volume. Principally, music, sound effects, etc., when taken down, form a background for a main sound or speech, or suggest that the music, etc., is being distanced from the microphone (audience).

ECU. extreme closeup. More rare terms for the same are XCU, and BCU (big closeup).

ELS. extreme long shot (sometimes abbreviated Ext. LS). Often synonymous with the term Cover shot.

Epilogue. (1) brief unit of a drama, outside of the plot proper and following the plot's resolution. (2) Concluding dramatic explanation. Sometimes used in teleplays, seldom in motion pictures.

Establishing shot. a view of the general scene; usually a long shot, it sets the scene in locale, shows characters in spatial relation to one another, and establishes season, time of day, etc. An establishing shot is usual when shifting from one locale to another or when introducing a new sequence.

Exposition. material informing the audience of what had gone before, if necessary to the understanding of the story.

EXT. exterior. An exterior scene, or one which purports to have been shot out-of-doors. Each new scene in cinema is usually specified as to interior or exterior.

Fade in. (1) an optical effect in which each successive frame of film, starting from black, is given more and more exposure until the scene is finally raised to its full, normal exposure. The connotation of fades is that a change of place and/or a major change of time is occurring. They are often likened to an act curtain (rather than a scene curtain) in theatre, as regards time/place change. (2) In sound, an increase in volume from silence to an acceptable level.

Fade out. (1) opposite of the fade in: a gradual transition from the normally exposed image to final blackness. (2) In sound, a decreasing level of volume until inaudibility.

Fast motion. filming at less than 24 frames-per-second (the standard projection rate), so that the screened action will appear more rapid than it had actually occurred. The camera will be said to have been undercranked, in achieving the effect. Sometimes called accelerated motion.

Feature. (1) to emphasize an object or a character (as in, "Feature the doorway," or, "Angle featuring Fred"). (2) A full-length theatrical film, either dramatic fiction or documentary, which plays anywhere from 100 to 170 minutes.

Filmograph. a motion picture featuring copied still photographs or art rather than "live action."

Filter. (1) in sound, the elimination or modification of certain frequencies for purposes of reducing sibilants, creating "telephone" or ethereal effects, eliminating harshness, etc. (2) Visually, any modification of the image by means of toned or treated material situated in front of the camera or printer lens. Filters can change the color of objects being filmed, can lessen the amount of light passing through the lens, can soften the image, can add a foggy quality, or create a sparkly effect.

Flashback. a narrative device in which a scene depicting an occurrence of the past is inserted into a sequence of "present" time. Sometimes, the entire body of the drama is presented as in the past, with the present merely a frame for it.

Flash cutting. use of shots of only a few frames each: they may follow each other in succession (in the manner of montage) but are usually used as inserts in a scene to infer remembrance or, sometimes, future action. Sometimes called flutter cutting.

Flash-forward. opposite of flashback; scenes of the future. As a narrative device, the flash-forward is less comprehensible to audiences, and more difficult for the artist to clarify, than is the flashback.

Flutter cutting. (see Flash cutting).

Follow focus. manually altering the focus of the camera lens from one spatial plane to another as the shot progresses, so as to maintain focus of a subject as it advances toward or recedes from the camera. (To follow focus is not always necessary optically, nor is it mandatory dramatically.)

Follow shot. (see Dolly shot).

Format. (1) gauge of filmstock or other recording material (super 8, 16 mm, 35 mm, ¼-inch, etc.). (2) A broadcast operation's type of programming (all-news, MOR, country & Western, B-movies, etc.). (3) The form of a script, or the type of program. (4) A program's plan of principal features; its outline; particularly, the scripting of these particular features (including the opening, closing, and transitions throughout the program body) with mere indications of the remaining aspects of the program.

Freeze-frame. an optical effect in which one frame of film is repeated many times, giving the illusion that the action is frozen in time, or that the action has suddenly become a still photograph. The connotation of the freeze-frame (beyond its possible values of transforming motion into a studiable static tableau) is that the objects/subjects in the frame have become memorialized, or have passed into another plane, apart from the "naturalism" of motion.

Front projection. similar in effect, but superior in results, to the process screen. An image which shares the same axis (within 5 degrees latitude) with the camera lens is projected onto live actors and the highly reflective screen before which they stand; because of the high reflectance of the screen and the bright lighting of the actors, no projected image is visible on the actors or their props.

Full shot. a shot which includes the principle subject and little else; the filling of the frame by an entire figure.

Gimmick. (1) a plot device, particularly one which aids the resolution of the drama's problem. (Related to the term Plant.) (2) In TV, that kind of program which hinges upon some off-beat object or condition (i.e., a genie's bottle, a talking car, a robot policeman, a bionically reconstituted athlete, etc.).

Hold. (1) to freeze; often, to freeze either camera or subject. (2) Indication of a stop position for drawings or pan backgrounds when they are being photographed in animation. (3) In audio, to hold is to maintain at the same level, or to establish a level of volume (as in, "Take music down and hold behind the narration").

Hook. (see Teaser).

ID. (see Station identification).

Insert. a detail shot giving specific information relevant to the scene; a close, explanatory addition.

INT. interior. (See EXT.)

Intercut. inclusion of visual material not part of the present sequence.

Jump cut. a time-bridge caused by the elimination of inessential portions of motion within a scene. A jump cut calls attention to the craft of cinema, and is usually a disturbing, jarring effect. Often it is an unintentional result of ineptitude, but it may also be calculated and purposeful.

Lap dissolve. an obsolete term for dissolve in cinema, although television personnel may use the word "lap" as a verbal cue to dissolve from one picture to another.

Library shot. (see Stock shot).

Lip sync. (from "synchronization") in film, the precise matching of speech with lip movement or,

consequently, of any sound with the object which produced it.

Live tag. an addition by an announcer to a recorded message in radio or TV, so as to close the announcement with information of a local nature, such as local dealer and address, local price, local time, etc. (See also Tag.)

Logo. (1) a designed visual symbol. (2) An advertiser's identification trademark, or the station's or network's identification (e.g., the CBS eye, the MGM lion, etc.).

Long shot. (1) a visual overview; an open, orienting angle. (2) In the case of a single figure, the inclusion of the entire figure plus some margin above and below. (3) A shot which distances the audience from the action. Often synonymous with full shot. (Abbreviated LS.)

LS. (see Long shot and ELS).

MacGuffin. a suspense device: the term as used by Alfred Hitchcock means a dramatic element (gimmick) which secures audience attention and/or drives the plot forward, while having little or nothing to do with the essentials of the story.

Master scene script. in film, a script which, while including complete dialogue, narration, etc., describes rather large and cohesive action units rather than delineating shot details or specifying exact camera angles.

Master shot. (1) coverage of an entire action in a single shot. (2) Usually a LS running the entirety of a scene.

Match cut. (1) the joining of two shots the second of which contains some element(s) of the previous shot. (In this regard, the opposite of the cut-away.) (2) Often, the term refers to the joining of nearly identical compositions or actions, as a time/place bridge (e.g., in *The Quiet One*, the camera moves in to a CU of a white tablecloth being spread, followed by a match cut to identical white as the camera moves out to reveal a stack of white dishes newly washed).

Matte shot. a shot made for purposes of a special (optical) effect: it is of extreme contrast, having clear areas to allow print-through of some picture portions, and opaque areas to prevent print-through of the remainder of the picture. When printed with a regular shot, it masks portions of the action and allows another scene to be printed in the masked-off area, thus allowing a combination of two scenes' elements into one scene.

Medium shot. a shot from a middle distance; between CU and LS. In the case of a single figure, the medium shot includes the head and torso, revealing use of the hands. Sometimes (though rarely) called a mid-shot. (Abbreviated MS.)

Miniature. (see Model shot).

Mise-en-scene. (1) character in context; actors (performances, make-up and costumes) and setting (props and lighting) combining to create an impression. (2) Qualities generated by this combined impression (approximately synonymous, visually, with the term style). (3) Sometimes used as the opposite of montage, since long takes with camera movement and actor movement are choreographed to achieve maximum effect.

Model shot. an "effects" shot of miniatures or models rather than real objects and/ or real locations; of special value in filming disasters or action of a sort which would preclude camera placement.

Monologue. (see Sound).

Montage. a succession of shots, generally rapid, containing the same idea or creating a concept through association of the shots. The shots in the montage are usually joined by cutting, but dissolves may also be used, as may (multiple image) superimposures and other optical effects. By its means, a general effect is created, such as the passage of time, a mood or mental condition, or the generation of an abstract idea.

MS. (see Medium shot).

Multiple exposure. double, triple, or more complex images superimposed onto the same strip of film (thus, not to be confused with split screens, multi-image projection, etc.). A kind of nonlinear montage.

Music. (see Sound).

Narration. (see Sound).

Negative image. opposite of conventional images; in the negative image blacks are transparent (white), whites black, and colors appear as their complements.

Obligatory scene. (1) that which the audience "demands to see." (2) As a part of dramatic structure, the event the viewer is led to believe will be the climax, which it usually immediately precedes. The pivotal character is seen in a positive or negative situation toward which the plot has seemed to point. (3) Therefore, that which fulfills expectations of the audience and the characters.

Off mike. nonalignment with a microphone's optimum pickup pattern, causing a distancing effect. (The aural convention is that the audience is where the microphone is; the off mike voice

or sound is therefore assumed to be some little distance away.)

Off-screen narration. commentary from an unseen source (see Voice-over and OS).

Optical. anything accomplished in the lab, rather than on the set or in the editing room, which alters the presentation of the image. Opticals include fades, dissolves, wipes, freeze-frames, matte shots (see these terms), etc.

OS. (1) "out of the shot," or "off screen": the voice of a player who is temporarily off-screen. The term voice over is not precisely synonymous with OS, because voice over refers to commentative speech by a presenter seldom or never seen. (2) Also may be used to mean an over-the-shoulder shot.

Outline. (1) version of a script or idea proposal written prior to a detailed treatment. (2) General sketch of the subject and story content of the production. (3) The synopsized idea, presented in essay form rather than as a script or in numerized layout.

Overcrank. (1) to expose more motion picture frames per second than the standard 24. Overcranking results on the screen as a slowed, smoothed, serene action. (2) Opposite of undercrank or fast motion. (Note also Slow motion.)

Overlap sound. (1) result of picture and sound not being cut at the same instant; sound extending from one shot into the next, in which it does not "logically" belong, or sound from the following scene bridging the cut from the preceding scene. Used to forecast or to create an association between a visual and a sound which usually would not accompany it. (2) In radio, TV, or film, therefore, a kind of transitional element.

Over-the-shoulder. basically a two-shot, with the camera revealing at least the back of the head and a shoulder of one player while featuring the other, frontally positioned, player in proximity to him. (May be abbreviated OS.)

Pan. (1) pivoting of a stationary camera along a horizontal axis. (2) Literally, abbreviation of "panorama." (See also Tilt).

Pay off. in dramaturgy, the bringing into play of a previously planted object or, more rarely, a character or an idea. If the antagonist smashes a bottle and, later, one of its fragments is used by the protagonist to sever his bonds and escape, the broken glass is a plant and the cutting of the ropes by means of it is the pay off.

Pedestal. a vertical move created by raising or lowering the camera by means of a cylinder mount on a special dolly.

Pixilation. (1) a version of animation in which stationary objects appear to be in motion by reason of a slight movement of them or their parts between single exposures (frames). (2) A less frequently employed method of pixilation involves the printing only of selected frames, in order, from an already filmed action.

Plant. (see Pay off).

Plot. (1) the basic plan of a drama. (2) The chronological arrangement of a script's structural elements in the general order of: the revelation of the conflict; the joining of the conflict; the presentation of crises and reversals; the obligatory scene; the climax; and, finally, the denouement.

Point of view. (1) a writer's stance, or that which he purports. (2) The camera's (viewer's) angle toward the action. The points of view are objective (in which audience is spectator without direct involvement), performer's (in which audience is not directly involved but is in a position nearly identical with that of the performer), and subjective (in which the audience "participates" psychologically as though the lens is its eyes and the witnessed events are consequently personal). (Abbreviated POV.)

POV. (see Point of view).

Premise. (1) a central idea, usually generated by a hypothetical question, which sets the creation of a story in motion. (2) A suggestion, in prose form, for a drama (see Synopsis).

Process screen. method whereby an image (still or motion) is projected from behind onto a translucent screen before which performers carry out their action, resulting in the appearance of the performers being somewhere they are not. Use of the process screen saves money (compared to on-location work), precludes risk in otherwise dangerous circumstances, and optimizes sound recording in situations otherwise difficult or impossible to control. Nevertheless, it is now subordinate in use to the newer and more efficient front projection. Sometimes called process photography, and, in TV, rear screen, rear projection, or back projection.

Prologue. (1) brief unit of a drama, outside of the plot proper and prior to its commencement. (2) Introductory explanation; a "setting of the scene." More often used in teleplays (where it frequently functions as a teaser) than in screenplays.

Protagonist. the force, usually embodied in a character, with which the audience aligns its sympathies and about whose fate it becomes most concerned.

Pull back. (1) to track or zoom back from the action. (2) To move out to a wider, more revealing view.

Rack focus. camera technique using a shallow focus in which that focus is shifted from one spatial plane to another. To rack focus is to lead the eye of the viewer from one place to another in depth, since the eye seeks out sharply focused and avoids fuzzily focused objects. Sometimes called shift focus.

Reaction shot. a view away from the main scene to something related and in close proximity to it; a reaction shot shows response to action, rather than the actual occurrence itself.

Rear projection. (see Process screen).

Reel. a period of screen time (ten to eleven minutes) consumed by the running of a 400-foot spool of 16mm film or a 1,000-foot spool of 35mm film. Thus, nine or more reels constitute a theatrical feature-length film.

Relief. a scene planned to reduce audience tension by humor or other means, following a heavily dramatic or exciting sequence.

Resolution. (1) the solution of a drama's principal problem. (2) The final outcome of the conflict faced by the protagonist; the result of the drama's climax.

Reversals. (commonly called "reversals of fortune") as a part of dramatic structure, the high points of each crisis; as the protagonist seems about to achieve his goal, he suffers an unexpected setback, a reversal, so that he must try again by another means, which in turn leads to a further obstacle. In well-conceived drama, reversals are not made up only of action, but are profound moments because, through the experiences they provide, the protagonist usually comes to understand something about himself, thus adding important dimension to his character and, consequently, heightening audience interest in him.

Reverse angle. (1) without transpositioning objects, the camera is moved or pointed in a direction nearly opposite to its former position or angle (thus, for example, the performers are shown first from the front and second from the rear, allowing the display of different backgrounds for the same subject). (2) Reverse also includes the technique of showing, say, a minister looking left, followed by his listening congregation looking right.

Reverse motion. backward playing of an action, accomplished by running the film backward through the camera during photography or, more commonly, by producing a film copy in an optical printer which reproduces frames 1, 2, 3, 4, etc., as frames 4, 3, 2, 1. The effect of reverse motion is that time and event move backward.

Running gag. humor produced by repetition or embellishment of an incident or behavioral detail through the course of a presentation.

Scenario. film story in the form of scenes and sequences, but not in precise detail. Nearly synonymous with the term screenplay.

Scene. (1) the equivalent of literature's paragraph; one or more shots in a single location, and dealing with the same action. The scene is a numbered section of a script. (Note also Sequence and Shot.) (2) Theatrically, any addition or subtraction of a character: on his exit, for instance, the scene ends. This use of the term is rarely used in media.

Screenplay. film story in outline or script form, although seldom detailed in the manner of a shooting version. Nearly synonymous with the term scenario. The range of usage of screenplay as a term renders it ambiguous.

Script. a manuscript containing specifications of a presentation in any medium. (See Master scene script, Scenario, Screenplay, and Shooting script.)

Segue. an audio transition resulting from the flow of one musical selection into the next until it replaces it; thus, the aural equivalent of the dissolve. Technically identical with the cross-fade.

Sequence. the equivalent of literature's chapter; a group of shots or scenes comprising one major expository statement.

Sequence outline. equivocal term often used interchangeably with the terms treatment (although sometimes more detailed) and outline. A developed presentation, not in script form, of an idea for a film, indicating visual as well as aural content.

Set-up. a positioning of the camera, usually to include placement of lights and ancillary preparation for the shot or scene.

Shallow focus. narrow range of optical sharpness before the camera (e.g., the middle ground may be sharp, and the foreground and background blurred); thus, opposite of deep focus. Often dramatically valuable because it concentrates viewer attention on the principal subject. (See also Rack focus.)

Shift focus. (see Rack focus).

Shooting script. the final, production-ready version, containing detailed and specific angles, bits of business, etc. Reflects the changes called for by the director, designers, producer, and others.

Shot. the equivalent of literature's sentence; a single run of the camera. There are no cuts or optical transitions within a shot. May be thought of as a single pictorial composition unless there is motion of subject, camera, or both. (Note also Scene and Sequence.)

Silence. (see Sound).

Slide kit. a medium which uses a series of conventional 35mm slides, arranged in a pre-determined order and housed in any of several types of slide projector magazines. A presentation in this medium may be accompanied by an elaborate sound recording or by commentary read "live". The order of slides can be changed at will (new slides replacing less effective ones) at minimal cost.

Slow motion. (1) smoothed, retarded, languid motion resulting from exposing more than the standard 24 frames per second, usually 64 or more. Slow motion creates dream-like distortion of time and motion. Also useful in restoring a sense of proper "time scale" to miniatures during model shots, and in allowing study of motion too rapid to be apprehended adequately by the unaided eye. Slow motion can be said to be produced by overcranking the camera. High-speed cinematography is extreme slow motion: actual time decelerated 20 times, 125 times or even more. (2) In television, an equivalent effect is produced by a special scanning rhythm of a playback head across a magnetic disc.

Sneak. very slow fade of picture or of sound. The term is used primarily in TV and radio.

SOF. (see Sound-on-film).

Soft focus. a less than crisply sharp image caused by purposeful use of special lenses or filters in order to create a romantic effect or to otherwise soften the harshness of actuality.

Sound. aural elements of any of the media. Sound, collectively, is termed audio in TV. (Note also Filter.) Sounds may be grouped into four categories:

1. *Speech.* dialogue, narration, monologue, and rhetorical dialogue. Dialogue is the interchange of lines between two or more characters. Narration is commentative and usually off-screen, except in TV documentaries and the like. Monologue is the protracted verbalization of a character, as though speaking to himself. Rhetorical dialogue is a "solo" directly to the audience, a kind of one-sided conversation with the au-

dience, as though they could respond should they so choose. This is the conventional method of the on-screen TV commercial presenter.

2. *Music.* can predict coming events; can establish mood, or maintain and/or change it; can identify character qualities; can support or create tempo and movement; can provide a sense of locale; can indicate time; can heighten dramatic effect; and can function as a theme, as in the accompaniment to titles and credits. Note that there is no such thing, artistically, as "background music," but that music is aesthetic and functional when properly employed.

3. *Sound effects.* crickets of the night, a door slam, winds of the prairie, a cafe's clattering dishware, etc. In their ability to provide or enhance mood and to function in other ways similar to those cited for the music category, sound effects have values far beyond merely mirroring what can be seen. (May be abbreviated FX.)

4. *Silence.* the contrast against which sounds themselves operate. Often, silence is the most dramatically effective and powerful of all sound elements.

Sound-on-film. (1) a "wedded," or composite print (a screen-ready film copy having both picture and soundtrack). (2) A piece of film onto which the sound was originally and directly recorded during photography. (Abbreviated SOF.)

Split screen. combination of two or more scenes presented simultaneously on one screen. Unlike the multiple exposure, the split screen's images are not superimposures but complete and unaltered images relegated to their own sections of the frame. Split screens are often used to show a cause and its effect simultaneously, or the same act being done by two or more persons at once; it is commonly seen in the situation of the telephone conversation, where caller and answerer are both shown, or in TV commercials where an inset of the pitchman hovers near his product.

Stab. a musical exclamation point; the abrupt and startling insertion of a note, chord, or burst of short notes for dramatic effect.

Station identification. programming element occurring between programs or during extended programs. Usually referred to as a 10-second announcement (actually 8 seconds), it often reserves only 2 seconds for the station's call letters to be given, while the remaining 6–8 seconds are sold to an advertiser. In TV, the visual element of the identification is shared between the station's logo and call letters, and an advertiser's slogan, community message, holiday greeting, etc. (Abbreviated ID and also called Station break, or, sometimes, shared ID.)

Sting. a sudden, emphatic vocal or instrumental sound used for punctuation. (See Stab.)

Stock shot. (1) a shot originally made for another purpose and archived in a film repository from whence it can be obtained, usually for a fee; valued source material of otherwise difficult or impossible cinematography. (2) A secondary meaning of the term is derogatory: footage so mundane or so unimaginative that it indeed appears to have been obtained from an archive. Sometimes called Library shot.

Stop motion. operation of the camera one frame at a time, rather than at its normal 24 frames-per-second mode. In this operation, objects can be readjusted between frames resulting in "trick" effects.

Storyboard. a series of drawings resembling the panels of a comic strip which reveal the continuity of a presentation, including camera moves, transition methods, sound elements, and, most importantly, the composition of proposed shots. A valued communication tool in that it presents easily changeable visualizations of the proposal before more expensive aspects of production are undertaken, and also in that it makes the continuity and pictorialization more comprehensible. The storyboard may be presented as a "rough"—sketched visual suggestions—or, when more refined, as a "comprehensive" (or "comp") which is in color, with accurate highlights, shadows, background detail, etc. Some storyboard comps are sufficiently expressive and artistic to be filmed "off the sheet" as the actual visuals for, say, a commercial.

Subjective camera. (see Point of view—subjective).

Subplot. a story line enclosed within the principal story to provide relief from the main plot's tension, add character dimension, etc.

Superimpose. to overlay two or more images onto the same strip of film (or videotape) by means of camera or lab work. Particularly popular in titling, where the words are "burned in" against a pictorial background. (Abbreviated in TV as "super.")

Swish pan. a pan much too rapid to allow discerning of details along its path; a blur along a horizontal axis. Used to produce an abrupt transition and not to reveal spatial relationships or specific pictorial aspects. Less commonly called a whip pan, and sometimes zip pan or flick pan.

Synopsis. very brief (usually one page) summary of

a plot, suggesting aspects of content; similar to a book report, it is prepared from a finished script or a detailed treatment.

Tableau. static arrangement or grouping, usually of performers; motionless posing. Because it "represents," the tableau often possesses a significance. Dramatic freeze-frames produce tableaux.

Tag. (1) musical phrase to close a radio or TV program, or to conclude a major portion of same. (2) Music at the end of live copy to set one commercial apart from a following commercial. (3) A brief announcement at the end of a recorded commercial or service announcement, containing added, usually local, information. (4) A performer's final line, used to close a program (see also Live tag). (5) Final brief closing scene.

Take. (1) primary unit in shooting film: amount of action recorded during the interval between turning the camera on and turning it off. A take is a shot. In production, there are often two or more takes made of a given action, with the best being included in the finished film. (2) The term applies in the same way to music, narration or other sound recording. (3) Sometimes used to mean a surprised reaction, comic or otherwise (see Reaction shot).

Target audience. the specific group for which a presentation is designed, calculated as to age, sex, knowledge-level, etc.

Teaser. (1) form of program opening designed to present an enigma or other provocative material so as to induce the audience to stay tuned. (2) In TV dramatic or comedic forms, a kind of prologue which sets the situation while exciting interest. Therefore sometimes called a hook.

Telephoto. lens of very long focal length. Its effect is to make foreground, middle-ground and background appear closer together than they actually are, decreasing the illusion of depth and apparently increasing the time it takes for a subject to recede from or approach us. (Opposite of wide angle.)

Tempo. the pace of a presentation; the sense of forward movement it conveys.

Theme. the statement of the dramatic work: its thesis, message, emotional truth, expression of the nature of man. Audiences regard overtly verbalized themes as pontifical; in well-conceived dramatic work, the theme will be implicit and illustrated by character action.

Tilt. scanning up or down by a camera in stationary position; movement through the vertical plane.

Time-lapse. extreme fast motion: exposure of single frames, rather than the standard 24-per-second, so as to radically compress time (e.g., a rose buds, swells, and unfolds in only a few screen seconds). Time-lapse allows comprehension of materials which develop so slowly in actuality that they could not otherwise be observed.

Titles. screened information to be read by the audience and appearing either as separate graphics or as superimposures over picture. When the information acknowledges individuals' work, the title is a credit.

Track. (1) to move a camera toward, away from or at some angle to the action. (2) The "rails" for the camera carriage used in such a move. (See Dolly shot.) (3) A film's sound-bearing edge stripe. (4) Any of a film's several component sound recordings before they have been mixed into one composite.

Tracking shot. sidewise, forward or backward camera movement. (See Dolly shot, Follow shot, and Truck.) Also called traveling shot.

Transition. that which connects one segment of a presentation with the next, containing some element of both the outgoing and incoming segments. In visual media, optical effects, character movement, or camera movement are used as transitions. In the aural media, transitions are achieved by fades, cross-fades, segues, etc.

Treatment. content of teleplay or screenplay written in literary form; a general description of the program. It is one of the intermediary steps between an outline and the full screenplay. Often, sequences are indicated in the treatment.

Truck. parallel, backward or forward movement of the camera, usually dolly mounted, during a take; often used to keep a moving subject the same image size throughout the take.

Two-shot. inclusion of two figures, usually in loose medium shot; most common framing for dialogue takes.

Under. subordination of one or more sounds to a dominant (foreground) sound. Such subordinated sounds are said to be "taken under" or "held under."

Undercrank. to expose fewer film frames per second than the standard 24 (see Fast motion and Time-lapse). The effect of undercranking is to compress time because it speeds up motion.

Up. (1) prominence of one or more sounds over others. (2) Volume increase of a sound or sounds into the foreground. One is said to "take up" or "bring up," or "hold up," such sounds.

Video. (see Action).

VO. (see Voice over).

Voice over. narration or other spoken lines from an unseen source. (Abbreviated VO.)

Whip pan. (see Swish pan).

Wide angle. lens of short focal length. Its effect is to make foreground, middle-ground and background appear farther apart than they actually are, increasing the illusion of depth, and apparently abbreviating the time it takes for a subject to recede from or approach us. (Opposite of telephoto.) In closeups, foreground objects (noses, weapon muzzles, etc.) will appear distorted through disproportionate enlargement.

Wipe. optical effect in which an incoming image appears to push the outgoing image off the screen or to replace it from one corner of the frame to another, from top to bottom, from bottom to top, from the center outward, etc. It creates a transition through implications of cause-and-effect or other such relationship.

XCU. (see ECU).

Zoom. (1) optical effect created by a variable-focal-length lens or by optical printing, in which a subject is moved from CU to LS or vice-versa during a take. (2) Apparent movement, usually rapid, of subject toward or away from the camera. The zoom resembles a dolly shot, but appears more artificial because the subject, and not the viewer, seems to approach or retreat.